Math in Focus®
Singapore Math®
by Marshall Cavendish

Transition Guide

For New Program Implementation
and Intervention

Marshall Cavendish
Education

US Distributor

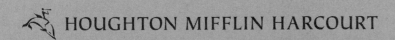
HOUGHTON MIFFLIN HARCOURT

COMMON CORE

Published by Marshall Cavendish Education
An imprint of Marshall Cavendish International (Singapore) Private Limited
Times Centre, 1 New Industrial Road, Singapore 536196
Customer Service Hotline: (65) 6411 0820
E-mail: tmesales@sg.marshallcavendish.com
Website: www.marshallcavendish.com/education

Common Core Standards © Copyright 2010.
National Governors Association Center for Best Practices and
Council of Chief State School Officers. All rights reserved.

This product is not sponsored or endorsed by the Common Core State Standards
Initiative of the National Governors Association Center for Best Practices and
the Council of Chief State School Officers.

Distributed by
Houghton Mifflin Harcourt
222 Berkeley Street
Boston, MA 02116
Tel: 617-351-5000
Website: www.hmheducation.com/mathinfocus

First published 2013

Math in Focus® Transition Guide Course 2
ISBN 978-0-547-61808-1

Printed in United States of America

6 7 8 1026 17 16 15
4500554817   A B C D E

Math in Focus®

Singapore Math®
by Marshall Cavendish

Introduction

The *Math in Focus® Transition Guide* provides a map to help transition teachers and students new to the *Math in Focus®* program.

Much of the success of Singapore math is due to the careful way in which algorithms are developed, with an emphasis on understanding. Lessons move from concrete models to pictorial and symbolic representations. Students develop mathematical ideas in depth, and see how the concepts are connected and that mathematics is not a series of isolated skills.

Teaching to Mastery With Student Proficiency

Singapore has been scoring at the top of international comparison studies for over 15 years. One of the key characteristics of the Singapore curriculum is teaching to mastery. This Transition Guide is designed to help teachers as they transition their students into *Math in Focus®*.

What Does Transition Mean?

Transitioning in *Math in Focus®* is the process of using specific methods to teach concepts and skills students have not yet mastered or been exposed to at previous grade levels, so they can attain mastery at their current grade level.

What is the Difference Between Transition and Intervention?

Transition is providing students with the needed exposure to topics and methods that were taught in the previous grade levels. Intervention is serving students who have had repeated exposure and lack mastery. The transition process is beneficial to students who require intervention.

Using the Transition Guide

- *The Transition Guide* Math Background addresses five critical strands: Number Sense (NS), Ratios and Proportional Relationships (RP), Expressions and Equations (EE), Geometry (G), and Statistics and Probability (SP). Additional Math Background support is provided at the beginning of each chapter in the *Math in Focus®* Teacher's Guide.

- The *Math Background* topics were chosen to help teachers understand and apply the Singapore approach upon which *Math in Focus®* is based. These topics are either introduced earlier than in other programs or are presented differently in this program.

- The classroom teacher can easily scan through the *Math Background* to determine the set of skills and concepts taught in prior years. Ensuring that a student has these background skills will help the student succeed in this program.

- For each skill objective, there are *Transition Worksheets*. These worksheets provide step-by-step instruction, practice, and review. A student can follow the steps independently or with someone's help. Corresponding teacher guides provide alternate teaching strategies, checks, and intervention suggestions.

- The *Transition Guide* is also available Online and on the Teacher One-Stop.

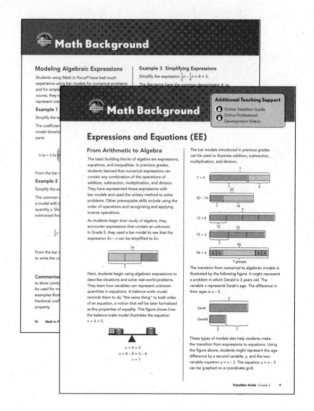

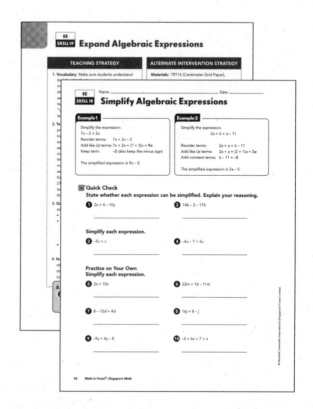

How does a teacher transition students? It's as easy as 1-2-3-4!

❶ Administer diagnostic test.

Use the items on the Chapter Pre-Test in *Assessments* book to determine whether a student has the necessary prerequisite skills for success in this chapter.

❷ Examine the diagnostic test for each student's strengths and weaknesses.

Use Recall Prior Knowledge and Quick Check in the *Student Edition* to review concepts and check for understanding.

❸ Determine the instructional pathway for each student.

Use the Resource Planner in the *Transition Guide* to find the appropriate Math Background and Skills worksheets.

❹ 🖱 Intervene, reinforce, and assess.

Use online *Reteach* and *Extra Practice* worksheets from one- or two-grades below.

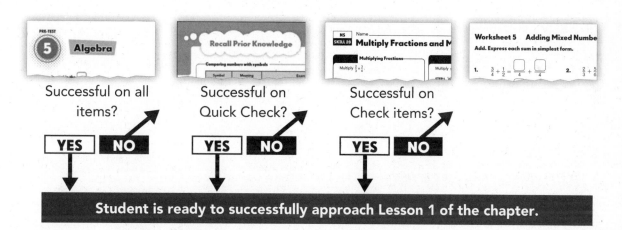

Successful on all items?   YES   NO

Successful on Quick Check?   YES   NO

Successful on Check items?   YES   NO

Student is ready to successfully approach Lesson 1 of the chapter.

Flexible Approach

Depending on your needs, you can also use the Recall Prior Knowledge Quick Check questions in the *Student Edition* to determine whether your students have the prerequisite skills for a chapter. The Chapter Pre-Test in the *Assessments* book can then serve as a check for understanding. You can also bypass Step 1 or Step 2.

Course 2 Contents

Course 2 Resource Planner

TRANSITION SKILLS AND RESOURCES

STRAND/ SKILL	SKILL OBJECTIVE	ASSESSMENTS PRE-TEST	STUDENT BOOK
NS 1	Recognize types of numbers.	Chapter 1: Items 1–2	Ch 1 RPK, QC 1
NS 2	Compare decimals.	Chapter 1: Items 3–6	Ch 1 RPK, QC 2–4
NS 3	Round numbers.	Chapter 1: Items 7–14	Ch 1 RPK, QC 5–13
NS 4	Find squares and square roots.	Chapter 1: Items 15–18, 23–24	Ch 1 RPK, QC 14–15, 18–20
NS 5	Find cubes and cube roots.	Chapter 1: Items 19–24	Ch 1 RPK, QC 16–20
NS 6	Determine absolute values.	Chapter 1: Items 25–27	Ch 1 RPK, QC 21–25
NS 7	Compare numbers on a number line.	Chapter 2: Items 1–6	Ch 2 RPK, QC 1–8
NS 8	Use order of operations to simplify numerical expressions.	Chapter 2: Items 7–8	Ch 2 RPK, QC 9-10
NS 9	Express improper fractions and mixed numbers in other forms.	Chapter 2: Items 9–12	Ch 2 RPK, QC 11-14
NS 10	Add and subtract fractions.	Chapter 2: Items 13–15	Ch 2 RPK, QC 15-17
NS 11	Multiply fractions.	Chapter 2: Items 16–17	Ch 2 RPK, QC 18–19
NS 12	Divide fractions.	Chapter 2: Items 18–19	Ch 2 RPK, QC 20-21
NS 13	Multiply decimals.	Chapter 2: Items 20	Ch 2 RPK, QC 22
NS 14	Divide decimals.	Chapter 2: Items 21	Ch 2 RPK, QC 23
RP 15	Use percents.	Chapter 2: Items 22–25	Ch 2 RPK, QC 24-27
EE 16	Recognize parts of an algebraic expression.	Chapter 3: Items 1–4	Ch 3 RPK, QC 1–4
EE 17	Evaluate algebraic expressions.	Chapter 3: Item 5	Ch 3 RPK, QC 5
EE 18	Simplify algebraic expressions.	Chapter 3: Items 6–13	Ch 3 RPK, QC 6–13
EE 19	Expand algebraic expressions.	Chapter 3: Items 14–17	Ch 3 RPK, QC 14–17
EE 20	Factor algebraic expressions.	Chapter 3: Items 18–21	Ch 3 RPK, QC 18–21
EE 21	Recognize equivalent expressions.	Chapter 3: Items 22–23	Ch 3 RPK, QC 22
EE 22	Write algebraic expressions for unknown quantities.	Chapter 3: Items 24–27	Ch 3 RPK, QC 23–26
EE 23	Solve algebraic equations by balancing.	Chapter 4: Items 1–4	Ch 4 RPK, QC 1–4
EE 24	Solve algebraic equations by substitution.	Chapter 4: Items 5–8	Ch 4 RPK, QC 5–8
EE 25	Graph inequalities on a number line.	Chapter 4: Items 9–12	Ch 4 RPK, QC 9–10

KEY: RPK (Recall Prior Knowledge), QC (Quick Check), C (Course)

⊙ ONLINE RESOURCES ONLY

C1 RETEACH	C1 EXTRA PRACTICE	GRADE 5 RETEACH	GRADE 5 EXTRA PRACTICE
C1A pp. 1–14	C1A Lesson 1.1		
C1A pp. 1–14	C1A Lesson 1.1	5B pp. 9–16	5B Lesson 8.2
		5A pp. 15–26, 5B pp. 9–16	5A Lesson 1.5, 5B Lesson 8.2
C1A pp. 28–29	C1A Lesson 1.4		
C1A pp. 30–32	C1A Lesson 1.5		
C1A pp. 41–44	C1A Lesson 2.2		
C1A pp. 33–40	C1A Lesson 2.1		
		5A pp. 63–70	5A Lesson 2.6
		5A pp. 95–104	5A Lessons 3.3, 3.4
		5A pp. 79–94, 105–112	5A Lessons 3.1–3.2, 3.5–3.6
		5A pp. 117–122, 129–130	5A Lessons 4.1, 4.3
C1A pp. 45–54	C1A Lesson 3.1	5A pp. 137–140	5A Lesson 4.6
C1A pp. 55–61	C1A Lesson 3.2	5B pp. 19–30	5B Lesson 9.1
C1A pp. 62–68	C1A Lesson 3.3	5B pp. 19–30, 39–56, 67–69	5B Lessons 9.3, 9.5
C1A pp. 165–179	C1A Lesson 6.5		
C1A pp. 180–184	C1A Lesson 7.1	5A pp. 143–146	5A Lesson 5.1
C1A pp. 185–186	C1A Lesson 7.2	5A pp. 143–146	5A Lesson 5.1
C1A pp. 187–193	C1A Lesson 7.3	5A pp. 147–152	5A Lesson 5.2
C1A pp.194–197	C1A Lesson 7.4		
C1A pp.194–197	C1A Lesson 7.4		
C1A pp. 187–197	C1A Lessons 7.3, 7.4		
C1A pp. 198–206	C1A Lesson 7.5	5A pp. 143–152, 157–158	5A Lessons 5.1, 5.2, 5.4
C1B pp. 1–15	C1B Lesson 8.1		
C1B pp. 1–15	C1B Lesson 8.1	5A pp. 153–156	5A Lesson 5.3
C1B pp. 27–32	C1B Lesson 8.3		

Course 2 Resource Planner

TRANSITION SKILLS AND RESOURCES

STRAND/ SKILL	SKILL OBJECTIVE	ASSESSMENTS PRE-TEST	STUDENT BOOK
EE 26	Write algebraic inequalities.	Chapter 4: Items 13–25	Ch 4 RPK, QC 11–18
RP 27	Compare quantities using a ratio.	Chapter 5: Items 1–2	Ch 5 RPK, QC 1–2
RP 28	Recognize equivalent ratios.	Chapter 5: Items 3–10	Ch 5 RPK, QC 3–8
RP 29	Find rates and unit rates.	Chapter 5: Items 11–13	Ch 5 RPK, QC 9–11
NS 30	Identify and plot coordinates.	Chapter 5: Item 14	Ch 5 RPK, QC 12
RP 31	Solve percent problems.	Chapter 5: Items 15–17	Ch 5 RPK, QC 13–15
G 32	Classify angles.	Chapter 6: Items 1–3	Ch 6 RPK, QC 1–6
G 33	Identify parallel lines and perpendicular lines.	Chapter 6: Items 4–7	Ch 6 RPK, QC 7–11
G 34	Classify triangles by side lengths.	Chapter 7: Item 1	Ch 7 RPK, QC 1
G 35	Classify triangles by angle measures.	Chapter 7: Item 1	Ch 7 RPK, QC 1
G 36	Name quadrilaterals.	Chapter 7: Item 2	Ch 7 RPK, QC 2
G 37	Use a protractor to measure an angle in degrees.	Chapter 7: Items 3–6	Ch 7 RPK, QC 3–6
G 38	Use a protractor to draw angles.	Chapter 7: Items 7–9	Ch 7 RPK, QC 7–10
G 39	Use a protractor to draw perpendicular line segments.	Chapter 7: Items 10–12	Ch 7 RPK, QC 11–13
G 40	Apply surface area and volume formulas for prisms.	Chapter 8: Items 1–3	Ch 8 RPK, QC 1–3
G 41	Find the surface area of a square pyramid.	Chapter 8: Item 4	Ch 8 RPK, QC 4
G 42	Find the area and circumference of a circle.	Chapter 8: Items 5, 6	Ch 8 RPK, QC 5–6
G 43	Identify nets of prisms and pyramids.	Chapter 8: Item 7	Ch 8 RPK, QC 7
SP 44	Find the mean of a set of data.	Chapter 9: Items 1–5	Ch 9 RPK, QC 1–5
SP 45	Find the median of a set of data.	Chapter 9: Items 6–10	Ch 9 RPK, QC 6–10
SP 46	Draw frequency tables and dot plots.	Chapter 9: Items 11–12	Ch 9 RPK, QC 11–12
RP 47	Express part of a whole as a fraction and a percent.	Chapter 10: Items 1–3	Ch 10 RPK, QC 1–3
RP 48	Express a fraction as a percent.	Chapter 10: Items 4–7	Ch 10 RPK, QC 4–6
RP 49	Express a percent as a fraction or decimal.	Chapter 10: Items 8–15	Ch 10 RPK, QC 7–14
RP 50	Express a ratio as a fraction or percent.	Chapter 10: Items 16–17	Ch 10 RPK, QC 15–16
SP 51	Solve a histogram problem.	Chapter 10: Items 18–20	Ch 10 RPK, QC 17

KEY: RPK (Recall Prior Knowledge), QC (Quick Check), C (Course)

ONLINE RESOURCES ONLY

C1 RETEACH	C1 EXTRA PRACTICE	GRADE 5 RETEACH	GRADE 5 EXTRA PRACTICE
C1B pp. 33–39	C1B Lesson 8.4	5A pp. 143–146	5A Lesson 5.3
C1A pp. 85–91	C1A Lesson 4.1	5A pp. 171–174, 191–198	5A Lessons, 7.1, 7.6, 7.7
C1A pp. 92–104	C1A Lesson 4.2	5A pp. 175–180, 183–190	5A Lessons 7.2, 7.4, 7.5
C1A pp. 117–126	C1A Lesson 5.1		
C1B pp. 64–67	C1B Lesson 9.1	5B pp. 103–106	5B Lesson 11.2
C1A pp. 156–164	C1A Lesson 6.4	5B pp. 87–96	5 B Lessons 10.3–10.4
		5B pp. 115–128	5B Lessons 12.1, 12.2, 12.3
		5B pp. 129–132	5B Lesson 13.1
		5B pp. 139–142	5B Lesson 13.3
		5B pp. 147–152	5B Lesson 13.5
C1B pp. 133–142, 143–146	C1B Lessons 12.2, 12.3	5B pp. 163–164, 169–182	5B Lessons 15.1, 15.3–15.5
C1B pp. 96–106, 107–112	C1B Lessons 11.1, 11.2		
C1B pp. 127–132	C1B Lesson 12.1	5B pp. 153–158	5B Lesson 14.1
C1B pp. 123–142	C1B Lesson 12.2		
C1B pp. 181–188	C1B Lesson 14.1		
C1B pp. 190–198	C1B Lesson 14.2		
C1B pp. 157–169	C1B Lesson 13.2	5B pp. 97–102	5B Lesson 11.1
C1A pp 142–147	C1A Lesson 6.1	5B pp. 81–86	5B Lesson 10.2
C1A pp 148–151	C1A Lesson 6.2	5B pp. 73–80	5B Lesson 10.1
C1A pp 148–151	C1A Lesson 6.2	5B pp. 73–80	5B Lesson 10.1
C1A pp 148–151	C1A Lesson 6.2	5B pp. 81–86	5B Lesson 10.2
C1B pp. 170–180	C1B Lesson 13.3		

The Number System (NS)

The Rest of the Real Numbers

Course 1 completed the study of numeration and computation through fractions and decimals. Students learned to represent positive and negative numbers on a number line. Now, in Course 2, the number line becomes the principal visual model. Students learn that whole numbers, fractions, decimals, and integers are also called rational numbers, which are a subset of the real numbers.

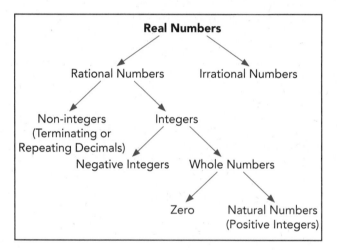

Why are number lines used so frequently in early lessons on integers, rational numbers, and irrational numbers? This one-dimensional coordinate system provides a method of representing all real numbers. All whole numbers, fractions, decimals, square roots, —even irrational numbers such as π and e —have a place on the real number line. That is, the real numbers and the points on the number line are in one-to-one correspondence.

Singapore math lays the groundwork for the real number line in earlier grades. Then students used this model to order and round whole numbers and decimals, as shown in the next diagrams.

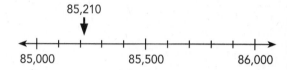

85,210 rounded to the nearest thousand is 85,000.

Although whole numbers and decimals can be shown with place-value charts, grid models are more appropriate for fractions. Notice how this model from an earlier grade connects a grid representation with the number line.

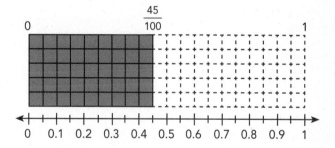

The following model, used for ordering fractions, illustrates the comparison of rational numbers in fraction and decimal forms.

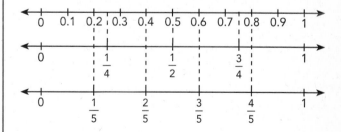

Math Background

(PROFESSIONAL LEARNING)

Representations of Real Numbers

The set of real numbers consists of two subsets—rational numbers and irrational numbers. Any number that can be written as the ratio of two integers is rational. The whole number 5 is rational, because it can be written as the ratio $\frac{5}{1}$. Any repeating decimal can be written as a ratio: $\frac{2}{3} = 0.666\ldots$ and $\frac{4}{11} = 0.363636\ldots$. In earlier grades, students learned to find the absolute value of integers. Now they see that a number line can illustrate the absolute value of other rational numbers.

Example 1 Write Mixed Numbers as Fractions

Write $-5\frac{3}{8}$ in $\frac{m}{n}$ form, where m and n are integers.

Change the mixed number to an improper fraction.

$$-5\frac{3}{8} = -\left(\frac{5 \times 8}{8} + \frac{3}{8}\right)$$
$$= -\left(\frac{40}{8} + \frac{3}{8}\right)$$
$$= \frac{-43}{8} \text{ or } \frac{43}{-8}$$

Example 2 Write Rational Numbers as Repeating Decimals

Write the rational number $\frac{11}{6}$ as a repeating decimal. Divide the numerator by the denominator. Keep dividing until the digits in the quotient show a repeating pattern.

$$2\overline{)11.000} \qquad \frac{11}{6} = 1.8\overline{3}$$
(quotient 1.833)

Example 3 Absolute Value

Find the absolute value of $-\frac{15}{16}$ and $\frac{43}{25}$.

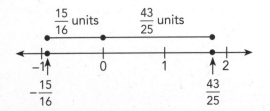

The absolute value of a number is its distance from 0.

$$\left|-\frac{15}{16}\right| = \frac{15}{16} \text{ and } \left|\frac{43}{25}\right| = \frac{43}{25}$$

Commentary The real number line helps to illustrate properties of real numbers, such as the order property of real numbers. If two real numbers a and b are not equal, then one must be less than the other.

Example 4 Compare Rational Numbers

Compare the numbers $\frac{32}{9}$ and $\frac{29}{8}$ using < or >. Use a number line to help you.

Change each fraction to a decimal.

$$\frac{32}{9} = 32 \div 9 = 3.\overline{5}$$
$$\frac{29}{8} = 29 \div 8 = 3.625$$

Draw a number line and mark the locations of the two decimals.

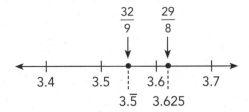

On the number line, 3.625 lies to the right of $3.\overline{5}$, so $3.625 > 3.\overline{5}$ and $\frac{29}{8} > \frac{32}{9}$.

Commentary Any set of three real numbers illustrates the betweenness property. For the real numbers a, b, and c, exactly one of them is between the other two. And, given two real numbers, there is always another real number between them. Students learn and apply order and betweenness properties as they use number lines to compare positive and negative rational numbers.

Computation with Integers and Rationals

Once students have a basic understanding of the real number system, they are ready to extend their computational skills to integers and rational numbers. They begin by using number lines and two-color counters to add integers with different signs.

Example 5 Adding Integers

Evaluate –8 + 3.

To use a number line, start at 0 and move 8 units in the negative direction. From this point at –8, move 3 units to the right in the positive direction. The final location is at –5, so –8 + 3 = –5.

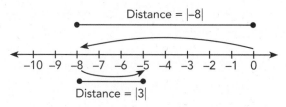

To add with counters, show –8 with 8 dark blue counters and +3 with 3 light blue counters. Remove three zero pairs. The final model shows the sum, –5.

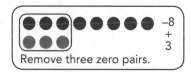

Commentary Integer subtraction is introduced with two-color counters and then formally developed as the addition of opposites. Number lines are used to illustrate a new interpretation of subtraction—the distance between two points.

$$1 - (-5) = 6$$

Commentary Students have previously learned the defining properties of the real numbers: the commutative, associative, identity, inverse and distributive properties. As they extend their number knowledge to include negative fractions and decimals, they will see that these properties continue to hold. The order of operations is another familiar concept that is now extended to real numbers.

Example 6 Order of Operations with Integers

Evaluate the expression.

$$-3 \cdot (6 - 10) + (-5)$$

First evaluate within the parentheses. Next, multiply. Then add.

$$-3 \cdot (6 - 10) + (-5)$$
$$= -3 \cdot (-4) + (-5)$$
$$= 12 + (-5)$$
$$= 7$$

Commentary Once students know the strategies for integer computation, they are ready to combine these ideas with what they learned in previous grades about computation with fractions and decimals.

Example 7 Multiply Rational Numbers

Find the product $1\frac{5}{6} \cdot -4\frac{1}{5}$.

First write each mixed number as an improper fraction.

$$1\frac{5}{6} \cdot -4\frac{1}{5} = \frac{11}{6} \cdot \left(-\frac{21}{5}\right)$$
$$= \frac{11 \cdot (-21)}{6 \cdot 5}$$
$$= \frac{11 \cdot (-7) \cdot \cancel{3}}{2 \cdot \cancel{3} \cdot 5}$$
$$= \frac{11 \cdot (-7)}{2 \cdot 5}$$
$$= -\frac{77}{10}$$
$$= -7\frac{7}{10}$$

Approximating Irrational Numbers

Real numbers that are not rational are irrational. Irrational numbers include all non-repeating non-terminating decimals, such as 0.1010010001..., the square roots of non-perfect squares, and transcendental numbers such as π and e. Students can find approximate locations for irrational numbers by choosing appropriate intervals with rational endpoints.

Example 8 Graph Irrational Numbers

Graph $\sqrt{55}$ on the number line using rational approximations.

Find an approximate value for $\sqrt{55}$ by using a calculator.

$\sqrt{55} \approx 7.4161985$

$\sqrt{55}$ is between 7.4 and 7.5. It is closer to 7.4.

Example 9 Order Real Numbers

Order this list of real numbers from least to greatest using the symbol <.

$$-\frac{15}{8}, \frac{\pi}{2}, -\sqrt{17}, \frac{13}{9}, -2\frac{3}{16}$$

Represent each real number in decimal form with 4 decimal places.

$-\frac{15}{8} = -1.8750 \qquad \frac{\pi}{2} \approx 1.5708 \qquad -\sqrt{17} \approx -4.1231$

$\frac{13}{9} \approx 1.4444 \qquad -2\frac{3}{16} = -2.1875$

Write the original numbers in order.

$$-\sqrt{17} < -2\frac{3}{16} < -\frac{15}{8} < \frac{13}{9} < \frac{\pi}{2}$$

Commentary Example 9 shows the use of rational approximations for ordering a set of real numbers. Students will usually represent irrational numbers by these approximations in computations and problem solving, so it is appropriate at this point for them to learn how to use significant digits.

Example 10 Identify Significant Digits

List the significant digits for each number.
1.4067, 0.0073, 2.650

1.4067
All non-zero digits are significant.
Zeros in between non-zero digits are also significant.
1, 4, 0, 6, 7

0.0073
Zeros to the left of the first non-zero digit are NOT significant.
7, 3

2.650
Trailing zeros in a decimal are significant.
2, 6, 5, 0

Example 11 Round To a Given Number of Significant Digits

Round 0.03285 to 2 significant digits.

The first two zeros are not significant.
Round the number to the nearest thousandth.
The third significant digit is 8, which is greater than 5.

$0.03285 \rightarrow 0.033$

Commentary Course 3 will continue the work with real numbers, as students learn to apply the laws of exponents and work with numbers in scientific notation. In later courses, they will learn about numbers besides the real numbers, such as imaginary numbers, complex numbers, and perhaps even the infinite ordinal numbers that are part of the surreal numbers.

Additional Teaching Resource

For additional reading, see *The Singapore Model Method for Learning Mathematics* published by the Ministry of Education of Singapore and *Bar Modeling: A Problem-Solving Tool* by Yeap Ban Har, published by Marshall Cavendish Education.

Ratios and Proportional Relationships

From Ratios and Rates to Proportional Reasoning

In previous grades, students were introduced to ratios as expressions for comparing quantities, but the many possible interpretations for an expression such as $\frac{2}{3}$ will be new. Depending on the context, $\frac{2}{3}$ can mean a fractional part of a set or a whole, the ratio 2 to 3, a rate such as 2 miles in 3 minutes, or the probability of rolling 5 or 6 on a number cube. This ratio also has three symbolic representations: $\frac{2}{3}$, 2 to 3, or 2 : 3.

Singapore math employs bar models and the unitary method. Bar models have the great advantage that they work as well for three or more part ratios as for two-part ratios. Here, for example, is a model showing 150 divided in the ratio 5 : 2 : 1.

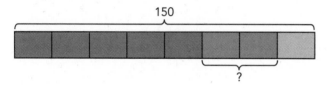

Since a percent is a special type of ratio—one with 100 as the second term—bar models and the unitary approach work effectively with percent problems.

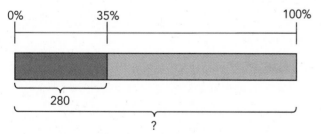

The model above can help students answer a question such as, "If 35% of the students at a school are eighth graders, and there are 280 eighth graders at the school, how many students are there in all?"

Another type of ratio is a rate, or a comparison of measures with different units. If the second term shows 1 unit, then the expression is a unit rate. The next model might be used for a problem about motion at the rate, or speed, of 18.5 miles per minute.

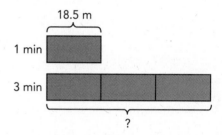

In this course, students take the next step, transitioning to tables that show equivalent rates.

Time (x hours)	2	3	4
Distance (y miles)	100	150	200

When the rates in a table are equivalent, the quantities are in direct proportion. For this table, the ratio of y to x is 100 to 2, or 50 to 1.

The ratio of the quantities in the table can also be represented by the equation $\frac{y}{x} = 50$. The more general form $\frac{y}{x} = k$ represents any direct proportion in which k is the constant of proportionality. Students learn that the graph of a direct proportion is always a straight line through the origin. In contrast, an inverse proportion has an equation of the form $xy = k$. For first-quadrant solutions, inverse proportions have curved graphs that do not intersect either axis.

In Course 3, students will continue to expand their knowledge of proportional relationships. They will learn to interpret the constant of proportionality as the slope of a direct proportion graph. They also will discover new applications for proportions.

Using Data Tables

Students begin by determining if a data table shows a direct proportion. When it does, they can find the constant of proportionality and represent the relationship with an equation.

Example 1 Identifying Direct Proportion

The table shows the cost for three amounts of the same product. Is c is directly proportional to x?

Number of Ounces (x)	8	16	48
Cost in Dollars (c)	1.28	2.56	6.72

To solve the problem, students must check all three ratios. For the relationship to be a direct proportion, all three must equal the same constant of proportionality.

Dividing the cost by the number of ounces results in the unit cost for each size.

$$\frac{1.28}{8} = 0.16 \qquad \frac{2.56}{16} = 0.16 \qquad \frac{6.72}{48} = 0.14$$

Because the unit cost is not constant, x and c are not in direct proportion.

Example 2 Interpreting the Constant of Proportionality

The table shows a plan for repairing roads in a small town. Find the constant of proportionality and tell what it represents. Then write a direct proportion equation.

Number of Weeks (x)	1	2	3
Miles of Road Repaired (y)	8	16	24

Constant of proportionality: $\frac{8}{1} = 8$

It represents the rate at which the road is being repaired, 8 miles per week.

The direct proportion equation is $y = 8x$.

Commentary Data tables provide a less abstract introduction to direct proportion than starting with equations such as $y = 8x$. The tables may remind students of data collection activities they have done for surveys and experiments.

Equations and Graphs for Direct Proportion

Once students understand the equation form and graphical properties of direct proportions, they can solve more abstract problems. For example, they will be able to determine that $2y = 15x$ shows a direct proportion, but $y - x = 10$ does not.

Example 3 Identifying Direct Proportion from a Graph

Tell whether the graph represents a direct proportion. If so, find the constant of proportionality and write a direct proportion equation.

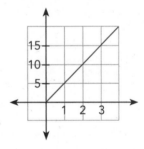

The graph is a straight line through the origin, so it shows a direct proportion. The graph goes through (1, 5), so the constant of proportionality is 5 and the equation is $y = 5x$.

Commentary In real-world applications, the graphed data may be discrete points. However, a straight line can still be drawn to show the proportional relationship.

Applications of Direct Proportion

Students' experiences with data tables and graphs create a solid conceptual foundation for understanding direct proportion. Then, students can apply direct proportion to a variety of problems.

Example 4 Direct Proportion and Percent

Last year 178 students competed in the science fair. This year, 24 more students have signed up for the fair. Use a proportion to find the approximate percent increase in the number of students.

$$x\% : 100\% = 24 : 178$$
$$\frac{x}{100} = \frac{24}{178}$$
$$100 \cdot \frac{x}{100} = 100 \cdot \frac{24}{178}$$
$$x = 13.5$$

There is an increase of about 13.5%.

Example 5 Using Cross-Multiplication

A student reads 14 pages of history in 35 minutes. If the student continues to read at the same rate, how long will it take her to read 100 more pages?

Write two ratios comparing the number of pages to the time in minutes.

$$\frac{14 \text{ pages}}{35 \text{ min}} = \frac{100 \text{ pages}}{x \text{ min}}$$
$$\frac{14}{35} = \frac{100}{x}$$
$$x \cdot 14 = 35 \cdot 100$$
$$14x = 3,500$$
$$\frac{14x}{14} = \frac{3500}{14}$$
$$x = 250$$

It will take 250 minutes, or a little more than 4 hours, to read 100 more pages.

Commentary Example 5 illustrates a common strategy. Students equate two ratios to make a proportion. Then they use cross products to write the proportion in a more familiar form.

In Singapore math, students are often shown multiple solution strategies. Direct proportion problems, such as Example 5, can also be solved by finding the constant of proportionality and writing a direct proportion equation. Compare the following solution strategy with the method used in Example 5.

Example 6 Using an Equation

A student reads 14 pages of history in 35 minutes. If the student continues to read at the same rate, how long will it take her to read 100 more pages?

Use the given information to find a constant of proportionality.

$$k = \frac{35 \text{ min}}{14 \text{ pages}}$$
$$= \frac{35}{14} \text{ minutes per page}$$
$$= 2.5 \text{ minutes per page}$$

Write the direct proportion equation. The variable x represents pages, and y represents minutes.

$$y = 2.5x$$

Find the number of minutes needed to read 100 pages. Substitute 100 for x and solve for y.

$$y = 2.5p$$
$$= 2.5 \cdot 100$$
$$= 250$$

It will take 250 minutes to read 100 more pages.

Inverse Proportion

Embedded in the concept of proportionality is the idea of variation. In direct proportion, also called direct variation, both quantities are increasing together. In contrast, inverse variation shows that one quantity decreases as the other increases. By checking the relationship between variables in a data table, students can determine if there is a constant ratio (direct proportion) or a constant product (inverse proportion).

Example 7 Identifying Inverse Proportion

Mr. Argula is planning the prizes for a math contest. The number of prizes will depend on the cost of each prize. The table shows some of his options.

Number of Prizes (x)	1	2	3	6
Value of Prize (y)	$60	$30	$20	$10

Tell whether y is inversely proportional to x. If so, find the constant of proportionality.

Find the product of each pair of values.

$$1 \cdot 60 = 60 \qquad 3 \cdot 20 = 60$$
$$2 \cdot 30 = 60 \qquad 6 \cdot 10 = 60$$

The product of x and y is the constant 60. As the number of prizes increases, the dollar value per prize decreases. So, the quantities are inversely proportional. The constant of proportionality is 60.

Commentary Once students can represent inverse proportion with equations, they can compare inverse proportions to direct proportions. In both defining equations, k is the constant of proportionality.

Direct Proportion $y = kx$ $\dfrac{y}{x} = k$

Inverse Proportion $y = \dfrac{k}{x}$ $xy = k$

The graph of an inverse proportion is curved rather than straight, and will approach each axis, but never intersect it. Students will learn later that these two axes are called asymptotes.

Example 8 Graphing Inverse Proportion

Jennifer has enough bricks to make a patio with a certain area. The area is fixed, so the length x and width y are inversely proportional. The graph shows how the length and width are related.

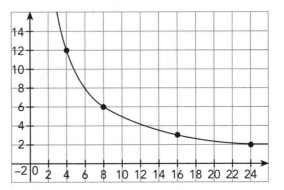

Find the constant of proportionality and interpret it in the context of the problem. Then write an inverse proportion equation.

Any point on the graph can be used for the constant of proportionality. A student might choose (8, 6).

$$8 \cdot 6 = 48$$

The constant of proportionality k is 48.

The fixed area must be 48 square yards.

The inverse proportion equation is $xy = 48$.

Additional Teaching Support

- Online Transition Guide
- Online Professional Development Videos

Expressions and Equations (EE)

From Arithmetic to Algebra

The basic building blocks of algebra are expressions, equations, and inequalities. In previous grades, students learned that numerical expressions can contain any combination of the operations of addition, subtraction, multiplication, and division. They have represented these expressions with bar models and used the unitary approach to solve problems. Other prerequisite skills include using the order of operations and recognizing and applying inverse operations.

As students begin their study of algebra, they encounter expressions that contain an unknown. In Grade 5, they used a bar model to see that the expression $3n - n$ can be simplified to $2n$.

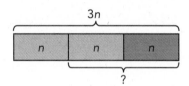

Next, students begin using algebraic expressions to describe situations and solve real-world problems. They learn how variables can represent unknown quantities in equations. A balance scale model reminds them to do "the same thing" to both sides of an equation, a notion that will be later formalized as the properties of equality. This figure shows how the balance scale model illustrates the equation $n + 4 = 5$.

The bar models introduced in previous grades can be used to illustrate addition, subtraction, multiplication, and division.

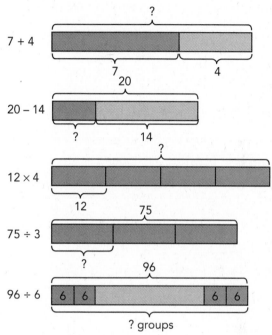

The transition from numerical to algebraic models is illustrated by the following figure. It might represent a problem in which Gerald is 3 years old. The variable x represents Sarah's age. The difference in their ages is $x - 3$.

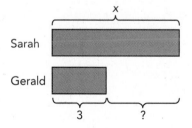

These types of models also help students make the transition from expressions to equations. Using the figure above, students might represent the age difference by a second variable, y, and the two-variable equation $y = x - 3$. The equation $y = x - 3$ can be graphed on a coordinate grid.

Modeling Algebraic Expressions

Students using Singapore math have had much experience using bar models for numerical problems and for simple expressions, such as $3n + n$. In this course, they now use models of the same type to represent coefficients that are rational numbers.

Example 1 Adding Like Terms

Simplify the expression $0.3a + 0.5a$.

The coefficients are tenths, so students draw a model showing the quantity a divided into 10 equal parts.

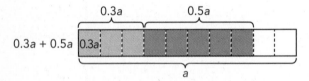

From the bar model, $0.3a + 0.5a = 0.8a$.

Example 2 Subtracting Like Terms

Simplify the expression $\frac{5}{6}y - \frac{1}{3}y$.

The common denominator is 6, so begin by drawing a model with 6 equal parts. The entire bar is the quantity y. Show 2 sixths (which equals 1 third) being subtracted from 5 sixths.

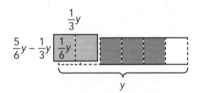

From the bar model, 3 sixths are left. The last step is to write the coefficient in simplest form.

$$\frac{5}{6}y - \frac{1}{3}y = \frac{3}{6}y = \frac{1}{2}y$$

Commentary Examples 1 and 2 use bar models to show combining like terms. Bar models also can be used for more complicated expressions. The next examples illustrate simplifying an expression with fractional coefficients and applying the distributive property.

Example 3 Simplifying Expressions

Simplify the expression $\frac{1}{2}n - \frac{1}{4}n + 8 + 3$.

The like terms have the common denominator 4, so the model shows n divided in 4 equal parts.

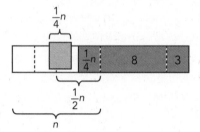

From the bar model, $\frac{1}{2}n - \frac{1}{4}n + 8 + 3 = \frac{1}{4}n + 11$.

Example 4 Expanding Algebraic Expressions

Expand the expression $\frac{1}{2}(2d + 6)$ using a bar model.

Start by modeling the expression inside the parentheses.

$2d + 6$ | d | d | 3 | 3 |

Rearrange the bar model into 2 equal groups. Draw a vertical dashed line to divide the groups in half.

$2d + 6$ | d | 3 | d | 3 |
$\frac{1}{2}(2d + 6)$

From the bar model, $\frac{1}{2}(2d + 6) = d + 3$.

Commentary Students will also use these models to factor expressions. In many of the examples, two methods are used, one with the visual representation and one that is purely symbolic. In a problem such as Example 2, Method 2 shows students how to subtract the coefficients and then simplify.

Equations and Inequalities

When students have multiple experiences creating and manipulating algebraic expressions, they can begin to write and solve equations with a much deeper understanding than with a rule-based approach. Equations are introduced by using a balance scale model to reinforce the concept of equivalent equations.

Example 5 Identifying Equivalent Equations

The balance scale model below shows two equations.

$$x - 3 = 5$$
$$x = 8$$

Are these equations equivalent? Explain.

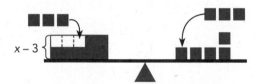

The model shows adding 3 counters to both sides. When this is done, the new equation is $x = 8$. Compare the solutions of the original equation and the new equation.

The solution of $x - 3 = 5$ is 8.
The solution of $x = 8$ is 8.

The solutions are the same, so the equations are equivalent.

Commentary The balance scale model is also used for two-step equations. Here, students solve $2x + 5 = 8$ by first removing 5 counters from both sides.

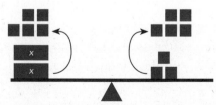

The idea of balancing can also be used for more difficult equations, such as those with rational number coefficients or variables on both sides. For more complicated problems, students are often presented with two methods, as in the next example.

Example 6 Solving Equations with Variables on Both Sides

Solving by balancing the equation.

Begin by adding $\frac{2}{3}x$ to both sides.

$$\frac{5}{6}x + 1 = 4 - \frac{2}{3}x$$
$$\frac{5}{6}x + 1 + \frac{2}{3}x = 4 - \frac{2}{3}x + \frac{2}{3}x$$
$$\frac{5}{6}x + 1 + \frac{4}{6}x = 4$$
$$\frac{9}{6}x + 1 = 4$$

Then continue to balance by subtracting 1 from both sides.

$$\frac{9}{6}x + 1 - 1 = 4 - 1$$
$$\frac{9}{6}x = 3$$

Finally, multiply both sides by the reciprocal of $\frac{9}{6}$.

$$\frac{6}{9} \cdot \frac{9}{6}x = \frac{6}{9} \cdot 3$$
$$x = 2$$

Commentary Example 6 shows the balancing method. In Method 2, students would begin by multiplying both sides of the equation by 6, the LCM of the denominators. The result is the equivalent equation $5x + 6 = -4x + 24$.

Many algebraic problems involve expressions that are not equal. Students begin their study of these inequalities by revisiting the balance scale model. This figure illustrates solving the inequality $x + 3 > 4$.

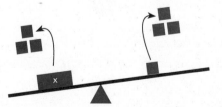

Students can then progress more easily to a more abstract model—representing solution sets on number lines.

Math Background

Real-World Applications

Before students can apply algebraic reasoning in problem situations, they need methods for translating verbal problems to symbolic notation. A diagrammatic approach called "translating by parts" provides a step-by-step strategy. This next example shows how students can use this approach to write an algebraic expression.

Example 7 Translating Verbal Descriptions

A team of 20 students win 12 prizes in a spelling bee. Each prize has a value of d dollars. The students share the prize money equally.

Write an algebraic expression for the amount of money each team member receives.

Total prize money	divided among	20 students
$12 \cdot d$	÷	20

$$\frac{12d}{20}$$
$$= \frac{3}{5}d$$

Each student receives $\frac{3}{5}d$ dollars.

Example 8 Using Bar Models And Algebraic Reasoning

Suzie is $\frac{1}{3}$ as old as her Uncle Mike. The difference in their ages is 36 years. Represent the problem two ways, first using bar models and then using algebraic reasoning.

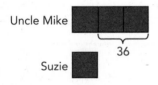

Let Uncle Mike's age be m. Then Suzie's age is $\frac{1}{3}m$. Write an equation showing the age difference.

$$m - \frac{1}{3}m = 36$$

Either way, Suzie's age is 18 and Uncle Mike's is 54.

Commentary Example 8 shows how students are presented with two methods for solving the same equation. In the first method, students apply the unitary approach to find the ages. In the second method, students solve for x to get Uncle Mike's age, and then use that value to find Suzie's age.

Students also see a variety of application problems for inequalities.

Example 9 Solving Problems Using Algebraic Inequalities

Alex got a $100 gift certificate for his birthday. He plans to buy a jacket for $45 and some T-shirts that cost $8 each. Find how many T-shirts Alex can buy.

Let x be the number of T-shirts Alex can buy.

$$45 + 8x \leq 100$$
$$45 + 8x - 45 \leq 100 - 45$$
$$8x \leq 55$$
$$8x \div 8 \leq 55 \div 8$$
$$x \leq 6.875$$

Alex can buy at most 6 T-shirts.

Commentary Although the primary emphasis in this course is on solving one-variable equations and inequalities, students will gain experience graphing two-variable equations in the chapters on proportional and statistical relationships. Course 3 provides complete coverage of graphing linear equations as well as equations for nonlinear functions. Students will also learn to solve systems of simultaneous equations both algebraically and by finding intersection points on graphs.

Additional Teaching Resource

For additional reading, see *The Singapore Model Method for Learning Mathematics* published by the Ministry of Education of Singapore and *Bar Modeling: A Problem-Solving Tool* by Yeap Ban Har, published by Marshall Cavendish Education.

Geometry

Synthetic and Metric Geometry

A significant portion of students' math studies does not involve numbers, variables, or equations at all. For example, the relationships among the quadrilaterals below can be discussed and analyzed without referring to any numerical information.

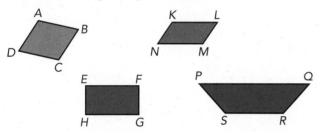

Ideas such as congruency (same size) or parallelism are independent of numbers. This type of geometry is called synthetic geometry. The figures are studied without reference to measurements. Compass and straightedge constructions introduced in Chapter 7 of this course are a part of synthetic geometry.

The basic properties and relationships about plane and solid geometric figures were the main focus in previous grades. As students classified angles, triangles, and quadrilaterals, they learned to use terms such as right, equilateral, scalene, acute, and isosceles to describe triangles such as these.

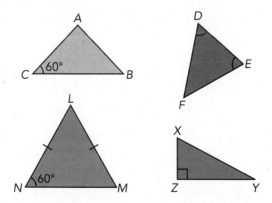

In Chapter 6 of this course, students explore properties of angle pairs, including angles formed by parallel lines and transversals.

Geometric figures can, of course, be connected with number concepts. In Course 1, students worked with figures on the coordinate plane. This prepares students for later topics in analytic geometry, such as the distance and midpoint formulas.

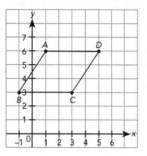 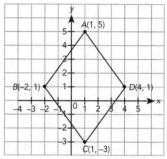

Metric geometry differs from synthetic geometry in that the measures of figures are important. All previous work with area, perimeter, circumference, volume, and surface area is a part of metric geometry. Course 1 concluded with the area and perimeter of plane figures. Here, for example, students find the areas of composite figures.

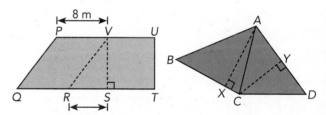

In Course 1, the solids that students studied were mainly prisms. Now, in Chapter 8, problems about volume and surface area deal with other figures—cones, pyramids, cylinders, and spheres.

The end of Chapter 7 includes problems on scale drawings. This prepares students for the material on similar figures in Course 3. Course 3 also focuses on translations, reflections, rotations, and dilations, as well as combinations of those transformations.

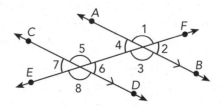

Math Background

Angle Properties

In previous grades, students learned to classify angles and triangles, and to identify pairs of lines as parallel, perpendicular, or intersecting. Now they will learn properties that involve two or more angles.

Example 1 Supplementary Angles

In the diagram, $\angle PQS$, $\angle SQT$, and $\angle TQR$ are angles on a straight line. Find m$\angle SQT$.

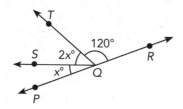

Since $\angle PQT$ is supplementary to $\angle TQR$, the sum of their measures must equal 180°.

$$m\angle PQT + m\angle TQR = 180°$$
$$m\angle PQT = 180° - m\angle TQR$$
$$m\angle PQT = 180° - 120°$$
$$m\angle PQT = 60°$$

Use the measure of m$\angle PQT$ to find x.

$$x° + 2x° = m\angle PQT$$
$$x° + 2x° = 60°$$
$$3x° = 60°$$
$$x = 20$$

Use x to find m$\angle SQT$.

$$m\angle SQT = 2x°$$
$$m\angle SQT = 2 \cdot 20°$$
$$m\angle SQT = 40°$$

Commentary Students learn that complementary angles have a sum of 90°, supplementary angles have a sum of 180°, and that vertical angles have equal measures. They apply these properties in many different situation. For example, they will determine congruent and supplementary angles that are formed when parallel lines are cut by a transversal, as in Example 2.

Example 2 Properties of Parallel Lines and Transversals

In the diagram, $\overleftrightarrow{AB}$ is parallel to $\overleftrightarrow{CD}$ and $\angle 1$ measures 135°. Find m$\angle 7$.

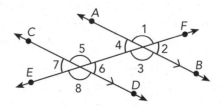

Angles 1 and 4 are supplementary, so the sum of their measures equals 180°.

$$m\angle 1 + m\angle 4 = 180°$$
$$m\angle 4 = 180° - 135°$$
$$m\angle 4 = 45°$$

Angles 4 and 7 are corresponding angles, so they are equal.

$$m\angle 7 = m\angle 4$$
$$m\angle 7 = 45°$$

Example 3 Exterior Angle Relationships

Find the value of x.

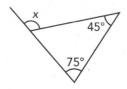

The exterior angle with measure $x°$ is supplementary to the unmarked interior angle of the triangle. That interior angle measure, plus the other two interior angle measures, also equals 180°. So, the measure of the exterior angle equals the sum of the measures of the two remote interior angles.

$$x° = 45° + 75° = 120°$$
$$x = 120$$

Commentary These examples show students that algebraic reasoning can be combined with geometric properties to solve problems. In Course 3, students will use these same skills as they explore congruence, similarity, and applications of the Pythagorean Theorem.

Constructions and Drawings

Creating figures using only a compass and unmarked straightedge was an important part of early Greek geometry. It is also important for students today. They learn basic constructions and how to use them, but they also discover relationships that always hold true. Students learn to reason deductively and make important conclusions about geometric figures, so that no measurement is required at all.

Example 4 Bisect an Angle

Draw an acute angle, ∠DEF. Construct the angle bisector using a compass and straightedge.

The completed construction is shown below.

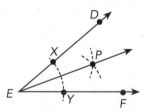

Students put the compass point at the vertex E, then draw the arc through points X and Y. Then they put the compass point at X and at Y and use the same radius to draw the arcs that intersect at P. The ray from E through P is the angle bisector. Every point on the angle bisector is equidistant from the two sides of the angle.

Example 5 Bisect a Line Segment

Draw a line segment labeled PQ. Construct the perpendicular bisector of segment PQ.

The completed construction is shown below.

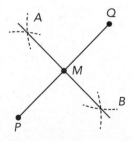

Students use the same radius to make the arcs shown at points A and B. The line through these points bisects segment PQ at the midpoint M. This construction is valid because of rhombus APBQ that is formed; the diagonals of a rhombus bisect each other and are perpendicular.

Commentary In some activities, protractors and marked rulers are used along with the compass and straightedge. Making use of all four tools simplifies the constructions so that students can focus on the underlying relationships. This figure illustrates the second-to-last step in constructing a parallelogram given two adjacent sides and an included angle.

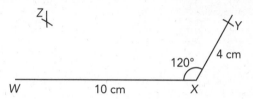

Students use the compass set at 4 cm, then set at 10 cm, to locate point Z.

Example 6 Draw a Triangle Given Two Angles and an Included Side

In triangle ABC, AB = 3 cm, m∠CAB = 40°, and m∠CBA = 60°. Use a ruler and protractor to draw triangle ABC.

The completed drawing is shown below.

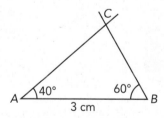

Students draw segment AB with a ruler, and then use a protractor for angles A and B. Rays AC and BC intersect to form the third vertex of the triangle.

Commentary As illustrated in Example 6, students also use geometric drawings to explore the triangle congruence relationships. In a full geometry course, they will learn the postulates and theorems used to prove that two triangles are congruent.

Three-Dimensional Figures

The use of nets as a way to construct and visualize solid shapes continues in this course as students learn about volume and surface area for cylinders, cones, spheres, and pyramids.

Example 6 Identifying Solids from Nets

Explain how each net relates to the solid it forms.

(a) 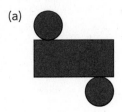   (b)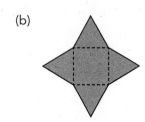

The first net forms a cylinder. The rectangle is rolled up and the two circles become the two bases.

The second net forms a square pyramid. The four triangles fold up and meet at the top vertex. The square in the middle is the base.

Commentary As students study volume and surface area, they contrast cylinders with cones and pyramids. A cylinder has a uniform cross-section so, like the prisms studied in Course 1, the volume equals the area of the base times the height.

The cross sections of cones and pyramids are not uniform, so the formula $V = Bh$ is not applicable. However, students learn by comparing the volumes of cones and pyramids to cylinders and prisms that cones and pyramids have an analogous formula for volume: $V = \frac{1}{3}Bh$.

The formulas for the surface area and volume of spheres have proofs beyond the scope of this course.

Commentary Students compute volumes and surface areas of solids and solve for missing dimensions such as height, radius, and slant height. This provides another instance in which algebraic skills are used in geometric contexts.

Example 8 Find the Radius of a Sphere from its Surface Area

A sphere can be covered with 4,000 square centimeters of canvas. Find the radius of the sphere, using 3.14 as an approximation for π.

The surface area of the sphere equals $4\pi r^2$. Substitute 4,000 for the surface area and solve for r.

$$4{,}000 \approx 4 \cdot 3.14 \cdot r^2$$
$$4{,}000 \approx 12.56 \cdot r^2$$
$$\frac{4{,}000}{12.56} \approx \frac{12.56 \cdot r^2}{12.56}$$
$$318.47 \approx r^2$$
$$\sqrt{318.47} \approx r$$
$$17.8 \approx r$$

The radius of the sphere is about 17.8 centimeters.

Commentary In Course 3, students will continue the work with composite solid figures. They also will learn how the Pythagorean Theorem is used to solve problems with cones, pyramids, and other solids. For example, in the figures below, the shaded right triangles illustrate how some dimensions satisfy the Pythagorean relationship.

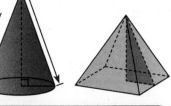

Additional Teaching Resource

For additional reading, see *The Singapore Model Method for Learning Mathematics* published by the Ministry of Education of Singapore and *Bar Modeling: A Problem-Solving Tool* by Yeap Ban Har, published by Marshall Cavendish Education.

Statistics and Probability (SP)

Analyzing and Representing Data

As early as Grade 4, students apply their newly-mastered skills in addition and division to find an average and, in so doing, learn that a single number can represent a set of data. In Course 1, average was introduced more formally as the mean. In addition, the measure of central tendency was expanded to include median and mode.

Now, in Course 2, the focus turns to measures of variation. Range, the difference between the least and greatest data set values, is familiar. Now students are introduced to quartiles and the interquartile range, learning that box plots are a good visual way to represent a 5-point summary: the upper and lower values, the upper and lower quartiles, and the median.

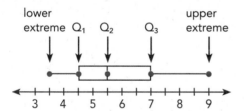

Students are then introduced to another measure of variation, the mean absolute deviation, which is the average distance of each data point from the mean.

In earlier grades, students collected and tabulated data. They used data displays such as frequency tables, double bar graphs, dot plots, and histograms. They also learned to describe the shape of a data set as symmetrical or skewed.

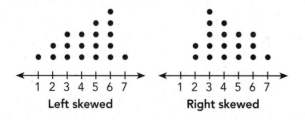

This course now explores data sampling in greater depth, including the idea of what is meant by a random sample. Then students make inferences from statistical data, both on single populations and as a way to compare two populations.

In Course 3, students will learn other methods for data representation and analysis: scatter plots, lines of best fit, and two-way tables for analyzing patterns in frequencies and relative frequencies.

Measuring Chance

Beginning in Grade 4, students learned that probabilities can be represented by fractions. In Grade 5, they learned the difference between theoretical and experimental probability. Experimental probability is based on data rather than theory. Sometimes it is used when a theoretical probability cannot be found, such as for predicting the weather or the color of the next car that passes. Also, it can be compared with theoretical probability. If students toss a coin many times, their results may or may not show "heads" and "tails" as equally likely outcomes, although theoretically they are.

Course 1 did not include probability, focusing instead on frequency distributions and measures of central tendency. In this course, students now use the ideas of outcomes, events, and sample space to compute probabilities for events. They work with pairs of events that are complementary or mutually exclusive. They learn that probability models can be used to estimate the probability of a chance event.

Course 3 will extend students' experiences with probability by covering compound events in greater depth and introducing the addition and multiplication laws.

Statistical Variation

Measures of variation are statistics that describe how data are spread out from the center. Describing the "center" and the "spread" of a data set are very important in data analysis. Students have learned several different measures for center (mean, median, mode). They will now learn several different measures for spread, which is also called variation.

Example 1 Display Data in a Stem-and-Leaf Plot

The data show the ages of people in a book discussion group: 48, 56, 30, 64, 67, 67, 41, 45, 48, 28, 31, 52, 32, 41, 28, 36

Display the data in a stem-and-leaf plot.

Book Group Ages

Stem	Leaf
2	8 8
3	0 1 2 6
4	1 1 5 8 8
5	2 6
6	4 7 7

2 | 8 represents an age of 28 years.

Commentary A stem-and-leaf plot can be used to find the extreme values as well as the mode and median. Note that either one or two data sets can be displayed on the same plot. This plot compares heights in centimeters in two groups of students.

Boys	Stem	Girls
8 5	17	7
9 8 7 1	18	1 6 8
9 7 2 0	19	1 3 5

17 | 7 represents 177.

Another measure of variation is the interquartile (IQ) range. It shows the spread of the middle 50% of the data. To find the IQ range, first identify the lower and upper quartiles. These are, respectively, the median of the lower half of the data and the median of the upper half of the data.

Example 2 Find and Interpret the Interquartile Range

Josh mails 15 packages. The weights, in ounces, are 8, 8.4, 10, 6.5, 7.4, 9.5, 5, 7, 8, 11, 6, 8, 7.2, 11.5, 7. Find the interquartile range for this data and interpret what it means.

List the weights in order. Draw a line through the median. Circle the lower and upper quartiles.

5, 6, 6.5, ⑦, 7, 7.2, 7.4, ⑧, 8, 8, 8.4, ⑨.⑤, 10, 11, 11.5

lower quartile Q_1 upper quartile Q_3

$$Q_3 - Q_1 = 9.5 - 7 = 2.5$$

The difference in the weights in the middle 50% of the packages is at most 2.5 ounces.

Commentary A box plot is a data display that shows both a center and measures of variability. The center is the median; the extreme values and the quartiles show spread. Unlike stem-and-leaf plots, box plots can show very large data sets. Two or more box plots are often displayed above the same horizontal axis, so that data sets can be easily compared.

Example 3 Comparing Data Sets with Box Plots

The populations of all the towns in two countries are compared on this box plot. Show that the two data sets have the same interquartile range.

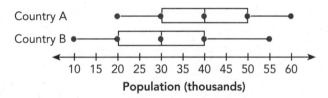

Country A $Q_3 - Q_1 = 50 - 30 = 20$
Country B $Q_3 - Q_1 = 40 - 20 = 20$

Both data sets have an IQ range of 20,000 people.

Sampling and Inference

Students have collected data in many ways: from counts or measures of an entire population; from simulations using physical models, calculators, or computers; and from experiments in both science and math classes. One other frequently used data-collection method is sampling. The sampling methods students learn in this course are all random.

Example 4 Use a Suitable Sampling Method

For each of the following scenarios, describe which sampling method you will choose and how you apply it. Justify your choice.

Scenario 1
A convenience store owner is trying to decide if she should sell fresh fruit. She decides to ask 50 customers.

A simple random sample is appropriate. Randomly choose 50 customers.

Scenario 2
A sports storeowner is deciding what kinds of winter jackets to have in stock. He decides to interview 100 customers.

Since the types of clothing are probably different for men and women, use a stratified random sample. Randomly choose 50 men and 50 women to interview.

Scenario 3
The city is checking trees along city streets for harmful insects. They estimate there are 1,200 trees and decide on a sample of 50 trees.

Use a systematic random sample.
Number the blocks with the trees to be checked.
Choose any tree at random in the first block.
Divide 1,200 by 50 to find the interval.
$1{,}200 \div 50 = 24$
Check every 24th tree.

Commentary Once students have learned some sampling methods, they are ready to apply their data representation and analysis skills to samples. Then inferences can be drawn from the sample data about the original and larger population. For example, they might find the mean and the mean absolute deviation for a sample. If the sample is representative, these measures can be estimated for the population.

Example 5 Use an Inference to Estimate a Population Mean

A population consists of 80 students. A random sample of 12 test scores {75, 80, 95, 70, 80, 95, 90, 80, 80, 65, 80, 95} was collected from the students.

Calculate the sample mean and use it to approximate the population mean. Then find the mean absolute deviation (MAD).

Add the 12 scores.
$75 + 80 + 95 + 70 + 80 + 95 + 90 + 80 + 80 + 65 + 80 + 95 = 985$

Divide by 12.
$985 \div 12 \approx 82.1$

The sample mean is about 82.1. So the population mean is estimated to be 82.1.

To find the MAD, calculate the distance of each value from the mean. Add these distances.

$7.1 + 2.1 + 12.9 + 12.1 + 2.1 + 12.9 + 7.9 + 2.1 + 2.1 + 17.1 + 2.1 + 12.9 = 93.4$

Divide by 12.
$$\text{MAD} = \frac{93.4}{12}$$
$$\approx 7.8$$

Commentary Students begin to learn about statistical inference by using sample statistics to estimate those measures for the population. In later courses, they will find ways to use probability to take chance variation into account. Probabilistic methods help ensure that different samples are unlikely to lead to different conclusions.

Math Background

Probability and Modeling

The terms *outcomes, sample space, event, and experiment* are basic to understanding probability. Once these terms are mastered, students can learn some of the terms that describe a pair of events. These include *mutually exclusive, not mutually exclusive,* and *complementary.*

Example 6 Favorable Outcomes and the Sample Space

A vending machine has apples, oranges, chips, protein bars, milk, and bottled water. *F* is the event of choosing a piece of fruit.

List the outcomes favorable to event *F*. State the number of outcomes in the sample space.

F = {apple, orange}
There are 6 types of items in the machine, so there are 6 outcomes in the sample space.

Example 7 Represent Non-Mutually Exclusive Events

Al, Bob, Cindy, and Dan are in the science club. Eve, Fred, and Greg are in the drama club. Hal belongs to both clubs. Irving and Jake are in neither club.

Let *X* be the event of randomly choosing a member of the science club. Let *Y* be the event of randomly choosing a member of the drama club. Draw a Venn diagram for the sample space.

One person is in both clubs, so the events are not mutually exclusive. Draw overlapping circles. Enclose the circles in a box so you can show the two people who are in neither club.

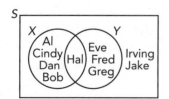

Commentary For a random variable, a probability model is the set of all possible values and the probabilities that each will occur. This relationship, like any other two-variable function, can be represented in tables or graphs. To begin to learn about probability distributions for these models, students first need some experience with relative frequency. Then they can use graphs to visually compare the difference between a uniform and a non-uniform probability model.

Example 8 Graph a Non-Uniform Probability Distribution

A group of 200 students were asked how long, to the nearest hour, they spent working on a science report.

Time (hours)	5	6	7	8
Number of Students	50	70	50	30

Construct a relative frequency table. Then graph the probability distribution.

Divide each value by 200 to find relative frequencies.

Time (hours)	5	6	7	8
Relative Frequency	0.25	0.35	0.25	0.15

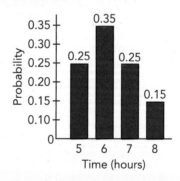

Additional Teaching Resource

For additional reading, see *The Singapore Model Method for Learning Mathematics* published by the Ministry of Education of Singapore and *Bar Modeling: A Problem-Solving Tool* by Yeap Ban Har, published by Marshall Cavendish Education.

Recognize Types of Numbers

TEACHING STRATEGY

1. **Vocabulary** Make sure students understand the term *interval* as it pertains to a number line. **Ask** If I want to show intervals of 1 on a number line between 0 and 10, where would the tick marks be placed? [0, 1, 2, 3, 4, 5, 6, 7, 8, 9, 10]

2. **Teach** Direct students to Step 1 of the Example. Tell them to look at the whole numbers and negative numbers. **Ask** What pattern do you see among the whole numbers and negative numbers? [The numbers increase or decrease by 2.] What does this pattern tell you? [Tick marks will be placed at intervals of 2.] In which direction from 0 on a number line would you place whole numbers? [right] In which direction from 0 on a number line would you place negative numbers? [left]

   Direct students to Steps 2 and 3 of the Example. Tell them that it may be helpful to place tick marks on the number line for values not listed in the chart. For example, they can place tick marks at intervals of 1. This will make it easier to graph the fractions and decimals.

3. **Quick Check** Look for these common errors as students solve the Quick Check exercises.
   - Incorrect placement of fractions due to problems comparing the values of fractions.
   - Incorrect placement of decimal values, resulting from errors converting decimal values to fractions or mixed numbers.

4. **Next Steps** Assign the practice exercises to students who show understanding. For students who need more support, provide tutoring using the alternate teaching strategy.

Additional Teaching Resource
Online Transition Guide with Reteach and Extra Practice worksheets from previous grade levels

ALTERNATE INTERVENTION STRATEGY

Materials: TRT 1(Number Lines), TRT2 (Number Cards 1–10), scissors, red markers

Strategy: Plot numbers on a number line.

1. Have students work in pairs. Give each pair blank number lines, four copies of Number Cards 1–10, scissors, and a red marker. Have students cut out the cards, then use the red marker to mark half the numbers on the cards to create a deck of mixed "red" and "black" number cards.

2. Explain that the value of each card is the number face on the card. Red-number cards represent negative numbers and black-number cards represent whole numbers.

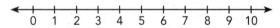

3. Use a number line like the one above.

4. Have each student draw a card from the deck and place a point on his or her number line where that number value belongs. Have students continue until each has plotted 5 numbers.

5. Repeat the process using decimals. Have students remove the 10s from their decks. They should draw 2 cards this time. The first card is the ones value and the second card is the tenths. Students should plot points on the number line to indicate the numbers they draw.

6. Repeat the process one more time using fractions. In this exercise, students draw 2 cards and write a proper or improper fraction using the numbers they draw. The first card drawn is the numerator and the second is the denominator. For example, if a student draws a 3 and then a 5, he or she writes the fraction $\frac{3}{5}$.

7. Have students create number lines with the appropriate labels and plot a point to indicate the fraction.

Name _____ Date _____

Recognize Types of Numbers

Example

Type of Number	Whole Numbers	Negative Numbers	Fractions	Decimals
Examples	0, 2, 4, 6	−2, −4, −6	$\frac{1}{2}$, $1\frac{3}{4}$, $\frac{16}{5}$	2.8, 5.75

Graph the numbers in the table on a horizontal number line.

STEP 1 Draw a number line from −6 to 6. Graph the whole and negative numbers.

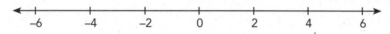

STEP 2 Graph the fractions. To help locate an improper fraction, convert it to a mixed number: $\frac{16}{5} = 3\frac{1}{5}$.

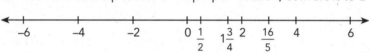

STEP 3 Graph the decimals. To help locate a decimal, you may want to convert it to a fraction or mixed number.

$$2.8 = 2\frac{8}{10} \qquad\qquad 5.75 = 5\frac{75}{100} = 5\frac{3}{4}$$

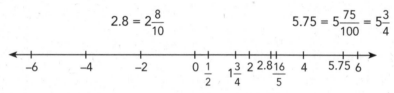

☑ Quick Check

Use the < symbol. Order the numbers from least to greatest.
Graph each number on a horizontal number line.

1 2.3, 0, −3, $\frac{1}{3}$, −1 _____

2 $\frac{8}{5}$, 0.5, $\frac{5}{4}$, 3, −2 _____

Practice on Your Own
Use the < symbol. Order the numbers from least to greatest.
Graph each number on a horizontal number line.

3 $\frac{17}{8}$, 0.8, 2.5, $\frac{1}{5}$, 1.8 _____

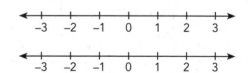

4 2.12, $\frac{18}{7}$, $\frac{1}{6}$, $1\frac{10}{17}$, $\frac{12}{13}$ _____

Compare Decimals

TEACHING STRATEGY

1. **Vocabulary** Review the symbols < (is less than) and > (is greater than) with students. Encourage volunteers to share whatever methods they use to distinguish between the two symbols.

2. **Teach** Explain to students that one way to compare decimals is by using a place value chart to compare digits in the same position in each number. Remind students that each place is one-tenth the value of the place to its left. Have students look at Example 1. **Ask** When comparing decimals, which place value should you start with? [the one that is farthest to the left] When can you stop comparing the digits in each number? Explain. [You can stop comparing when you find two different digits in the same place value. This tells you which decimal is greater.] Explain that you can also use a number line to compare decimals. Have students look at Example 2. **Ask** How does a number line help you compare decimals? [You can compare the numbers' positions on the number line. A number to the right of another number is the greater number.]

3. **Quick Check** Look for these common errors as students solve the Quick Check exercises.
   - Thinking that the decimal with more digits is greater, regardless of the place value of the digits.
   - Confusing the < and > symbols.

4. **Next Steps** Assign the practice exercises to students who show understanding. For students who need more support, provide tutoring using the alternate teaching strategy.

Additional Teaching Resource

 Online Transition Guide with Reteach and Extra Practice worksheets from previous grade levels

ALTERNATE INTERVENTION STRATEGY

Materials: TRT4 (Hundredths Grids); TRT5 (Place Value Charts)

Strategy: Use hundredths grids to compare decimals.

1. Write the decimals 1.09 and 1.7 on the board. Explain to students that they will use hundredths grids to model and compare the two decimals.

2. Shade 2 hundredths grids to model 1.09 for students. Then work with students to shade 2 hundredths grids to model 1.7. **Ask** How many squares do you need to shade in the first grid to model 1? [all 100] How many tenths are in 1.7? [7 tenths] How much of the grid do you need to shade to model 7 tenths? [Shade 70 squares or 7 columns.]

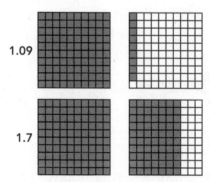

1.09

1.7

3. Have students compare the shaded portions of each model. **Ask** Which model has the greatest number of shaded squares? [the model for 1.7] Which number is greater? [1.7] Write the inequality 1.09 < 1.7 on the board.

4. Repeat the process for 0.34 and 0.18. Once students are comfortable with using the models, have them practice comparing the same decimals using place value charts and number lines.

Compare Decimals

Name _____ Date _____

Example 1 | Place Value Chart

Compare 1.53 and 1.57 using <, >, or =.

STEP 1 Write both decimals in a place value chart.

One		Tenths	Hundredths
1	.	5	3
1	.	5	7

STEP 2 Compare the values of the digits in each column in the chart, beginning at left and working to the right. Both decimals have the same values in the ones and the tenths places. In the hundredths place, 3 < 7. The value of 1.53 is less than the value of 1.57.

So, 1.53 < 1.57.

Example 2 | Number Line

Compare 1.53 and 1.57 using <, >, or =.

STEP 1 Draw a number line. Choose an interval that will allow you to plot points for all the numbers being compared.

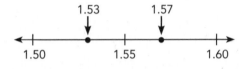

STEP 2 Plot the given values. On the number line, 1.57 lies to the right of 1.53. Therefore, 1.57 is greater in value.

So, 1.53 < 1.57.

✓ Quick Check

Compare each pair of numbers using <, >, or =. Use a place value chart or number line to help you.

1 1.326 ? 1.351

2 3.08 ? 3.17

3 0.489 ? 0.458

_____

_____

_____

Practice on Your Own
Compare each pair of numbers using <, >, or =. Use a place value chart or number line to help you.

4 12.05 ? 13.05

5 37.9 ? 39.7

6 10.3 ? 10.30

_____

_____

_____

7 9.4 ? 9.04

8 1.25 ? 1.31

9 100.7 ? 100.09

_____

_____

_____

10 5.055 ? 5.505

11 17.5 ? 17.50

12 10.6 ? 10.45

_____

_____

_____

Round Numbers

TEACHING STRATEGY

1. **Vocabulary** Make sure students can identify the place-value names from thousands to thousandths. Write 5,672.943 on the board. **Ask** What digit is in the tens place? [7] The hundredths place? [4] The thousandths place? [3] The ones place? [2] What is the place value of 5? [thousands] 9? [tenths] 6? [hundreds]

2. **Teach** Review the rounding process with students and work through the Examples. **Ask** What is the first step when rounding a number? [Identify the place you want to round to.] What is the next step? [Look at the digit to the right of the rounding place.] When do you round up? [When the digit to the right of the rounding place is greater than or equal to 5] When do you round down? [When the digit to the right is less than 5.] Make sure students understand how to round decimals with 9 in the rounding place. Work with students to round 20.998 to the nearest hundredth. Explain that the 9 hundredths will round up to 1 tenth. The 10 tenths will round up as 1 ones. So, 20.998 rounded to the nearest hundredth is 21.00.

3. **Quick Check** Look for these common errors as students solve the Quick Check exercises.
   - Looking at the rounding digit to determine whether to round up or down.
   - Keeping the digits to the right of the rounding place in the answer (e.g., rounding 2.67 to 2.77).

4. **Next Steps** Assign the practice exercises to students who show understanding. For students who need more support, provide tutoring using the alternate teaching strategy.

Additional Teaching Resource

🖱 Online Transition Guide with Reteach and Extra Practice worksheets from previous grade levels

ALTERNATE INTERVENTION STRATEGY

Materials: TRT5 (Place Value Charts)

Strategy: Use a place value chart to round numbers.

1. Display a place value chart showing thousands to thousandths and review the place values with students.

2. Write the number 6,371.298 in the chart and tell students you want to round the number to the nearest tenth.

thousands	hundreds	tens	ones	.	tenths	hundredths	thousandths
6	3	8	1	.	2	9	8

3. Review with students the steps for rounding a number. **Ask** What digit is in the tenths place? [2] What digit is to the right of 2? [9] Do you need to round up or down? [You need to round up.] Why? because 9 > 5] What should you do with the 2 in the tenths place? [Round the 2 up to 3.] What should you do with the digits in the hundredths and thousandths places? [Drop the digits.] What is 6,381.298 rounded to the nearest tenth? [6,381.3]

4. Work through a few additional examples with students. Then have students use their own place value charts to round the numbers below. Suggest to students that they highlight the rounding column in their charts to help them round the numbers correctly.

   12.492 to the nearest one. [12]
   3,761.5 to the nearest hundred. [3,800]
   4.063 to the nearest tenth. [4.1]

Name _____ Date _____

Round Numbers

Rounding a number provides an estimate of the number.

STEP 1 Find the place to which you are rounding.

STEP 2 Look at the digit immediately to the right of that place. For example, when rounding to ones, look at the digit in the tenths place.
- If this digit is greater than or equal to 5, then round up the digit in the rounding place by 1.
- If this digit is less than 5, then the digit in the rounding place is unchanged.

STEP 3 If you are rounding to a decimal place or to the nearest whole number, drop the digits to the right of the rounding place. If you are rounding to tens, hundreds, or any larger place value, then fill in zeros as needed.

Example 1 Next digit ≥ 5

Round 2,386.024 to the nearest ten.

2,386.024 8 is in the rounding place, tens. Look at the digit to its right, 6.

2,390 6 > 5, so round up 8 to 9. Fill in a zero for the ones place and drop the decimal digits.

2,386.024 rounded to the nearest ten is 2,390.

Example 2 Next digit < 5

Round 2,386.024 to the nearest tenth.

2,386.024 2 is in the rounding place, tenths. Look at the digit to its right, 4.

2,386.02 4 < 5, so do not change the 2 in the tenths place. Drop all the digits to the right of 2.

2,386.024 rounded to the nearest tenth is 2,386.02.

✔ Quick Check
Round 3,062.845 to each place indicated below.

1 to 2 decimal places

2 to the nearest ten

3 to the nearest whole number

_____   _____   _____

Practice on Your Own
Round each number.

4 4,285.7 to the nearest hundred

5 12.03 to the nearest tenth

_____   _____

6 64.48 to the nearest whole number

7 351.709 to the nearest hundred

_____   _____

8 0.076 to the nearest hundredth

9 109.95 to the nearest tenth

_____   _____

Find Squares and Square Roots

TEACHING STRATEGY

1. **Vocabulary** Make sure students understand the terms *base*, *exponent*, and *power*. Write 3^2 on the board. Explain that 3 is the base and 2 is the exponent. The exponent tells how many times the base is used as a factor. You read 3^2 as "3 raised to the second power" or "the second power of 3." Also, review the radical symbol ($\sqrt{\ }$) with students.

2. **Teach** Explain to students that the square of a number is the same as raising that number to the second power. Stress that squaring a number is not the same as doubling a number. **Ask** When you square a number, how many times is that number used as a factor? [twice] How do you find the value of 5^2? [Find the product of $5 \cdot 5 = 25$.] Point out that finding the square root of a number is the inverse of finding the square of a number. **Ask** How does knowing $5 \cdot 5 = 25$ help you find the square root of 25? [The square root of a number is a number that, when multiplied by itself, equals the original number. If $5 \cdot 5 = 25$, then the square root of 25 is 5.]

3. **Quick Check** Look for these common errors as students solve the quick check exercises.
   • Doubling a number instead of squaring it when raising the number to the second power.
   • Multiplying a number by the exponent, instead of multiplying the number by itself.

4. **Next Steps** Assign the practice exercises to students who show understanding. For students who need more support, provide tutoring using the alternate teaching strategy.

Additional Teaching Resource
 Online Transition Guide with Reteach and Extra Practice worksheets from previous grade levels

ALTERNATE INTERVENTION STRATEGY

Materials: TRT14(Centimeter Grid Paper)

Strategy: Use grid models to find the square and square root of numbers.

1. Explain to students that they can use grid paper to help determine the squares and square roots of numbers.

2. Instruct students to form a square by shading in 5 rows and 5 columns on the grid paper. Point out that this is a geometric representation of 5 "squared" because it forms a square with sides of 5 units.

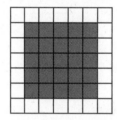

3. Have students count the number of shaded squares that make up the larger square. There are a total of 25 squares. **Ask** Aside from counting, how would you find the area of the larger square? [Multiply the length times the width: $5 \cdot 5 = 25$.] Connect this to the fact that 5 squared, or 5^2, is equal to $5 \cdot 5$ or 25.

4. Now explain to students that finding the square root of a number is the opposite of finding the square of a number. The square root of a number is a number that, when multiplied by itself, equals the original number. **Ask** Can you form a large square using 25 small squares? [Yes.] How many small squares make up one side of the larger square? [5] Connect this to the fact that $\sqrt{25} = 5$.

5. Have students repeat this exercise with 3 and 6. **Ask** What is 3^2? [9] What is 6^2? [36] What is $\sqrt{9}$? [3] What is $\sqrt{36}$? [6]

NS
SKILL 4 # Find Squares and Square Roots

The square of a number is its second power, or the product of the number and itself.

$$9^2 = 9 \cdot 9 = 81$$

The square root of a number is a number that produces the original quantity when multiplied by itself.

$$9^2 = 9 \cdot 9 = 81, \text{ so } \sqrt{81} = 9.$$

Squaring a number and finding the square root of a number are inverse operations.

Example 1 **Squares**

Find the square of 5.

STEP 1 Write a multiplication expression using 5 as a factor 2 times.

$$5 \cdot 5$$

STEP 2 Multiply to find the square.

$$5 \cdot 5 = 25$$

$$5^2 = 25$$

Example 2 **Square Roots**

Find the square root of 25.

STEP 1 Think: What number times itself is equal to 25?

$$n \cdot n = 25$$

STEP 2 Use your knowledge of multiplication facts to find the square root.

$$5 \cdot 5 = 25$$

$$\sqrt{25} = 5$$

✓ Quick Check

Find the square of each number.

1 3 _____

2 8 _____

3 16 _____

Find the square root of each number.

4 121 _____

5 16 _____

6 81 _____

Practice on Your Own
Find the square of each number.

7 7 _____

8 3 _____

9 10 _____

10 1 _____

11 6 _____

12 25 _____

13 13 _____

14 4 _____

15 17 _____

Find the square root of each number.

16 49 _____

17 9 _____

18 144 _____

10 576 _____

20 64 _____

21 225 _____

22 100 _____

23 400 _____

24 196 _____

Find Cubes and Cube Roots

TEACHING STRATEGY

1. **Vocabulary** Make sure students understand the terms *cube* and *cube root*. Write 2^3 and $\sqrt[3]{8}$ on the board and have students connect the expressions to the terms. If necessary, review the terms base and exponent.

2. **Teach** Explain to students that finding the cube of a number is the same as raising the number to the third power. Stress, however, that cubing a number does not mean multiplying the number by 3. **Ask** When you cube a number, how many times is the number used as a factor? [3] How do you find the value of 5^3? [Find the product of $5 \cdot 5 \cdot 5$.] What is the cube of 5? [125] Have students look at Example 2. Point out that finding the cube root of a number is the inverse, or opposite, of finding the cube of a number. **Ask** How does knowing $5 \cdot 5 \cdot 5 = 25$ help you determine the cube root of 125? [If $5 \cdot 5 \cdot 5 = 125$, then the cube root of 125 is 5.] To help students understand the relationship between cubing and finding a cube root, write $\sqrt[3]{n^3}$ on the board and demonstrate how one operation "undoes" the other one.

3. **Quick Check** Look for these common errors as students solve the quick check exercises.
   - Multiplying by 3 instead of cubing when raising a number to the third power.
   - A lack of mastery of multiplication facts, resulting in incorrect answers.

4. **Next Steps** Assign the practice exercises to students who show understanding. For students who need more support, provide tutoring using the alternate teaching strategy.

Additional Teaching Resource

🖱 Online Transition Guide with Reteach and Extra Practice worksheets from previous grade levels

ALTERNATE INTERVENTION STRATEGY

Materials: unit cubes

Strategy: Use unit cubes from the Manipulative Kit to find the cube and cube root of numbers.

1. Explain to students that they can use unit cubes to model the cubes and cube roots of numbers.

2. Instruct students to form 5 layers of cubes measuring 5 cubes by 5 cubes. Point out that this is a geometric representation of 5 "cubed" because it forms a cube whose dimensions are 5 by 5 by 5.

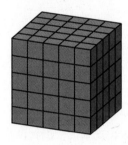

3. Have students count the number of individual cubes that they used to make the larger cube. There are a total of 125 squares. **Ask** Aside from counting, how would you find the area of the larger square? [Multiply the length times the width times the height: $5 \cdot 5 \cdot 5 = 125$.] Connect this to the fact that 5 cubes, or 5^3, is equal to $5 \cdot 5 \cdot 5$ or 125.

4. Now explain to students that finding the cube root of a number is the opposite of cubing a number. **Ask** Can you form a large cube using 125 small squares? [Yes.] How many small squares make up one side of the larger square? [5] Connect this to the fact that $\sqrt[3]{125} = 5$.

5. Have students repeat this exercise with 2 and 4. **Ask** What is 2^3? [8] What is 4^3? [64] What is $\sqrt[3]{8}$? [2] What is $\sqrt[3]{64}$? [4]

Name _____ Date _____

Find Cubes and Cube Roots

The cube of a number is its third power, or multiplying the number as a factor three times.

$$2^3 = 2 \cdot 2 \cdot 2 = 8$$

The cube root of a number is a number that produces the original quantity when multiplied as a factor three times.

$$3^3 = 2 \cdot 2 \cdot 2 = 8, \text{ so } = 2.$$

Cubing a number and finding the cube root of a number are inverse operations.

Example 1 Cubes

Find the cube of 5.

STEP 1 Write a multiplication expression using 5 as a factor 3 times.

$$5 \cdot 5 \cdot 5$$

STEP 2 Multiply to find the square.

$$5 \cdot 5 \cdot 5 = 25 \cdot 5 = 125$$

$$5^3 = 125$$

Example 2 Cube Roots

Find the square root of 125.

STEP 1 Think: What number can be used as a factor 3 times for a product of 125?

$$n \cdot n \cdot n = 125$$

STEP 2 Use your knowledge of multiplication facts to find the cube root.

$$5 \cdot 5 \cdot 5 = 125$$

$$\sqrt[3]{125} = 5$$

✔ Quick Check

Find the cube of each number.

1 4 _____ **2** 1 _____ **3** 10 _____

Find the cube root of each number.

4 27 _____ **5** 8 _____ **6** 512 _____

Practice on Your Own
Find the cube of each number.

7 3 _____ **8** 6 _____ **9** 2 _____

10 9 _____ **11** 7 _____ **12** 8 _____

13 15 _____ **14** 12 _____ **15** 20 _____

Find the cube root of each number.

16 216 _____ **17** 1 _____ **18** 729 _____

10 1,331 _____ **20** 64 _____ **21** 343 _____

22 1,000,000 _____ **23** 2,197 _____ **24** 27,000 _____

Determine Absolute Values

TEACHING STRATEGY

1. **Vocabulary** Make sure students understand the meaning of the term *distance*. Direct students to the number line in Example 1. **Ask** What is the distance between −4 and 0? [4] Direct students to the number line in Example 2. **Ask** What is the distance between −8 and 5? [13]

2. **Teach** Review the information at the top of the student page. Then work though Example 1 with students. Direct them to the number line. **Ask** As you measure the distance from 5 to 0, how many jumps do you make from unit to unit? [5] What direction do you jump? [to the left] If you measure the distance from 0 to 5, how many jumps do you make from unit to unit? [5] What direction do you jump? [to the right] Point out that distance is always positive. Then work though Example 2 with students. Write $|n| = -6$ on the board. **Ask** Can that statement ever be true? [No.] Why not? [The absolute value of a nonzero number is always a positive value.]

3. **Quick Check** Look for this common error as students solve the quick check exercises.
   - Writing negative absolute values for positive numbers, indicating that the student mistakenly believes the absolute value of a number is the opposite of that number.

4. **Next Steps** Assign the practice exercises to students who show understanding. For students who need more support, provide tutoring using the alternate teaching strategy.

Additional Teaching Resource
Online Transition Guide with Reteach and Extra Practice worksheets from previous grade levels

ALTERNATE INTERVENTION STRATEGY

Materials: TRT1 (Number Lines)

Strategy: Practice determining absolute values by using a table that compares the distance from 0 of pairs of opposite numbers.

1. Draw the table below on the board. Have students copy it on scrap paper.

Negative Value	Distance from 0	Positive Value
−3	[3]	3
−5	[5]	5
−7	[7]	7
−9	[9]	9
−11	[11]	11

2. Remind students that the absolute value of a number is the distance on a number line between that number and 0. Tell students that they are going to complete the center column by measuring the distance along a number line between the given values and 0.

3. Distribute blank number lines. Instruct students to label their number lines in whole-unit intervals from −11 to 11.

4. For each of the values in the table, instruct students to count the number of jumps (the distance) between that value and 0. Encourage students to make conjectures about the relationship between $|-n|$ and $|n|$. [They are equal.]

5. After students have completed the table, write several, random numbers less than −11 and several, random numbers greater than 11 on the board. **Ask** students to identify the absolute value for each number without using a number line.

NS
SKILL 6 # Determine Absolute Values

The absolute value of a number is the distance between that number and zero on a number line.
The absolute value of any nonzero number is always positive.

Example 1 Absolute Value Of a Positve Number

|5| is read as "the absolute value of 5."
|5| means the distance between 5 and 0 on a number line.

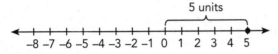

5 units

5 is 5 units away from 0.
So, its absolute value is 5.
|5| = 5

Example 2 Absolute Value Of a Negative Number

|–7| is read as "the absolute value of –7."
|–7| means the distance between –7 and 0 on a number line.

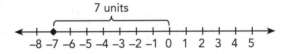

7 units

–7 is 7 units away from 0.
So, its absolute value is 7.
|–7| = 7

✔ Quick Check
Refer to the following set of numbers for questions 1–5.

16, –39, –62, 62, –63

1 Find the absolute value of each number. _____

2 Which number is closest to 0? _____

3 Name two numbers with the same absolute value. _____

4 Which number is farthest from 0? _____

5 Which number has the greatest absolute value? _____

Practice on Your Own
Refer to the following set of numbers for questions 6–10.

–76, 43, –93, –112, 113, –98, –121, 112

6 Find the absolute value of each number. _____

7 Which number is closest to 0? _____

8 Name two numbers with the same absolute value. _____

9 Which number is farthest from 0? _____

10 Which number has the greatest absolute value? _____

Compare Numbers on a Number Line

TEACHING STRATEGY

1. **Vocabulary** Students should be able to distinguish between the symbols > (is greater than) and < (is less than). Write the symbols on the board and have a volunteer explain what each symbol means. Encourage students to develop mnemonic devices to help them differentiate between the symbols, such as the symbols always point to the smaller number.

2. **Teach** Before working through the examples, make sure students understand how a number line can help them compare numbers.
Ask How can a number line help you compare two numbers? [You can locate two numbers on a number line and compare their values by comparing their positions on the number line.] On a horizontal number line, how do numbers increase in value? [The numbers increase in value from left to right.] On a vertical number line? [The numbers increase in value from bottom to top.] As you work through both examples, you may want to draw vertical number lines on the board to show students how to compare the numbers in each example on this type of number line.

3. **Quick Check** Look for these common errors as students solve the Quick Check exercises.
   • Misinterpreting the symbols > and <.
   • Misunderstanding the values of negative numbers.

4. **Next Steps** Assign the practice exercises to students who show understanding. For students who need more support, provide tutoring using the alternate teaching strategy.

Additional Teaching Resource

 Online Transition Guide with Reteach and Extra Practice worksheets from previous grade levels

ALTERNATE INTERVENTION STRATEGY

Materials: markers

Strategy: Use kinesthetic experience to compare numbers on a number line

1. Tell students that they will be working together to create a human number line to help them compare numbers.

2. Write –7 ? 2 on the board. Have 12 students come to the front of the classroom and form a line facing the room. Beginning with the student on the left, have each student identify the number they represent on the number line. The first student should begin with –8 and the last student on the right should end with 3. Make sure students remember to include 0 in their number line. Have each student write his or her numbers on a sheet of paper and hold it for the class to see.

3. Have the student who represents the number –7 step forward from the line. Then have the student who represents 2 do the same.

4. Have the class compare the two numbers by looking at the position of the two numbers on the number line. Remind students that numbers increase in value from left to right. So when you are comparing two numbers, the number furthest to the right is the greater number. **Ask** Which number is furthest to the right? [2] Is 2 greater than or less than –7? [greater than] **Ask** a volunteer to come to the board to replace the ? in the comparison you wrote with > or <. [–7 < 2]

5. Repeat this process using two negative numbers, two decimals, and two fractions.

NS
SKILL 7 # Compare Numbers on a Number Line

You can use a number line to help you compare numbers. On a horizontal number line, numbers increase in value as you move to the right. On a vertical number line, numbers increase in value as you move up.

Example 1

Use > or < to compare 2 and –5.

STEP 1   Draw a number line. Plot 2 and –5.

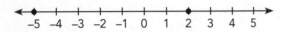

STEP 2   Compare the positions of the numbers. 2 lies to the right of –5, so it is the greater number.

2 > –5

Example 2

Use > or < to compare –0.75 and 0.25.

STEP 1   Draw a number line. Plot –0.75 and 0.25.

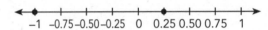

STEP 2   Compare the positions of the numbers. –0.75 lies to the left of 0.25, so it is the lesser number.

–0.75 < 0.25

☑ Quick Check

Complete each ▒ **with > or <.**

1 12 ▒ –8

2 –0.32 ▒ –1.55

3 $\frac{1}{3}$ ▒ $\frac{4}{5}$

_____

Practice on Your Own
Complete each ▒ **with > or <.**

4 –22 ▒ –3

5 $2\frac{1}{2}$ ▒ $-3\frac{1}{4}$

6 0.05 ▒ 0.95

_____

7 $-\frac{1}{3}$ ▒ $-\frac{1}{2}$

8 2.15 ▒ –2.68

9 3 ▒ –289

_____

10 –15 ▒ 15

11 $-\frac{3}{4}$ ▒ $-1\frac{1}{4}$

12 –10.88 ▒ –10.89

_____

Use Order of Operations to Simplify Numerical Expressions

TEACHING STRATEGY

1. **Vocabulary** Make sure students understand the term *order of operations*. Remind them that the order of operations is a set of rules that clarifies the order in which operations are carried out in an expression.

2. **Teach** Have students look at Example 1. **Ask** What operation should you perform first? [Add 12 and 6 in the parentheses.] What operation should you perform next? [Multiply 1 and 18.] What is the last operation you should perform? [Subtract 18 from 20.] Before working through the last two examples, **Ask** volunteers to list the operations they see in the problems, in the order in which they should be performed. Then write the expression $2 + 10 \cdot 3$ on the board and have students simplify it. **Ask** What is the correct answer? [32] What answer do you get if you work through the problem from left to right without following the correct order of operations? [36] Why do you think the order of operations is necessary? [If you don't follow the order of operations, you can get different values for the same expression.]

3. **Quick Check** Look for these common errors as students solve the Quick Check exercises.
   - Performing all operations from left to right as they appear in the expression.
   - Forgetting to perform the operations within parentheses first.

4. **Next Steps** Assign the practice exercises to students who show understanding. For students who need more support, provide tutoring using the alternate teaching strategy.

Additional Teaching Resource

 Online Transition Guide with Reteach and Extra Practice worksheets from previous grade levels

ALTERNATE INTERVENTION STRATEGY

Materials: none

Strategy: Explore how changing the order of operations changes the value of expressions.

1. Write the following numbers on the board: 2, 3, 4, 5 and 6. Tell students you are going to use each number exactly once, along with one set of parentheses and one each of the four operations $(+, -, \cdot,$ and $\div)$ to write an expression with a value of 4.

2. Write: $6 - (2 \cdot 3 + 4) \div 5$. Work through the correct order of operations to demonstrate that the result is 4.

$$6 - (2 \cdot 3 + 4) \div 5$$
$$= 6 - (6 + 4) \div 5$$
$$= 6 - 10 \div 5$$
$$= 6 - 2$$
$$= 4$$

3. Instruct students to repeat this exercise using the same numbers and the same rules to arrive at an answer of 3. Point out that they can have as many, or as few, numbers inside the parentheses are they need. Students may arrive at different results, but one possible result is $(2 + 3) \div 5 + 6 - 4$.

4. As students become more comfortable, mix up the operations. For example, require the use of two additions, two multiplications and no parentheses.

Sample problems:
1) Use the numbers 1, 2, 3, and 4 with one set of parentheses and one each of $+, \cdot,$ and $\div$ to arrive at a result of 8.
   [Possible answer: $4 \div 2 \cdot (3 + 1)$]

2) Use the numbers 2, 3, 4, 6, and 10 with one each of $+, -, \cdot,$ and $\div$ to arrive at a result of 11. No parentheses allowed.
   [Possible answer: $3 \cdot 4 + 10 \div 2 - 6$]

NS
SKILL 8

Use Order of Operations to Simplify Numerical Expressions

To evaluate an expression using the order of operations, follow these steps:

STEP 1   Perform operations within parentheses.

STEP 2   Evaluate exponents.

STEP 3   Multiply and divide from left to right.

STEP 4   Add and subtract from left to right.

Example 1

Evaluate $20 - 1 \cdot (12 + 6)$.

$20 - 1 \cdot \quad 18$

$20 - \quad 18$

Example 2

Evaluate $(9 + 21) \div 3 - 4$

$30 \div 3 - 4$

$10 - 4$

6

Example 3

Evaluate $9 \cdot 5 + 10 \div 5$

$45 \ + \ 2$

47

☑ **Quick Check**

Evaluate each expression.

1 $(2 + 4) \cdot 3 - 6$

_____

2 $(12 + 16) \div (19 - 12)$

_____

3 $3 \cdot 6 - 2 \cdot 9$

_____

Practice on Your Own
Evaluate each expression.

4 $(30 - 15) + 5 \cdot 8$

_____

5 $20 - (10 - 8) \cdot 6$

_____

6 $18 \div 2 + 6 \cdot 3$

_____

7 $12 \cdot 3 + (50 - 24)$

_____

8 $62 + 1 - 7 \cdot 8 + 1$

_____

9 $(2 \cdot 20) - 4 \cdot 10$

_____

10 $(30 - 8) \div 2 - 10$

_____

11 $20 + 6 - 2 \cdot 10$

_____

12 $21 + 72 \div 3 \cdot 2$

_____

13 $(5 + 4) + 16 \cdot 3$

_____

14 $7 \cdot 7 - 4 \cdot 9$

_____

15 $8 \cdot (5 + 6) + 23$

_____

Express Improper Fractions and Mixed Numbers in Other Forms

TEACHING STRATEGY

1. **Vocabulary** Make sure students understand the terms *improper fraction* and *mixed number*. **Ask** Is $\frac{7}{6}$ a proper or an improper fraction? Explain. [It is an improper fraction because the numerator is greater than the denominator.] Why is $\frac{4}{7}$ an example of a mixed number? [Possible answer: It combines a whole number and a fraction.]

2. **Teach** Work through Example 1 with students. **Ask** In Step 1, why is the numerator of $\frac{17}{5}$ written as the sum of 15 and 2? [You need to write the improper fraction as the sum of another improper fraction and a proper fraction. The numerator of the improper fraction has to be divisible by the denominator. In Example 1, 5 is a factor of 15, so the numerator is divisible by the denominator.] In Example 2, make sure students know how to rewrite the 3 as $\frac{21}{7}$. Remind students that when you add fractions with like denominators, you add the numerators and write the sum over the common denominator.

3. **Quick Check** Look for these common errors as students solve the Quick Check exercises.
   - Incorrectly breaking apart the numerator of the improper fraction, resulting in computation errors.
   - Mistakenly adding the denominator, the whole number, and the numerator in order to get the numerator of the improper fraction.

4. **Next Steps** Assign the practice exercises to students who show understanding. For students who need more support, provide tutoring using the alternate teaching strategy.

Additional Teaching Resource
Online Transition Guide with Reteach and Extra Practice worksheets from previous grade levels

ALTERNATE INTERVENTION STRATEGY

Materials: none

Strategy: Use models to express mixed numbers as improper fractions and improper fractions as mixed numbers.

1. Write on the board.

2. Draw a bar model to represent $\frac{17}{8}$. Point out that each bar is divided in eighths and explain that you need to draw enough bars to shade 17 parts. Point out to students that the shaded parts represent $\frac{17}{8}$. **Ask** How many whole bars are shaded? [2] What fraction represents the last model? [$\frac{1}{8}$]

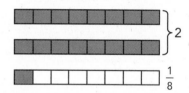

3. Have students combine the whole number and fraction to write the mixed number $2\frac{1}{8}$.

4. Work with students to develop a model for the mixed number $3\frac{2}{5}$. Explain that the denominator in the fraction, 5, tells you that the model must be divided into fifths. **Ask** How many fifths make 1 whole? [5] Draw one bar divided into fifths and shade all 5 parts. **Ask** How many wholes are in $3\frac{2}{5}$? [3] How many more models do I need to draw to show 3 wholes? [2] Draw one last fifths bar and shade 2 of the parts to represent $\frac{2}{5}$.

5. **Ask** How many fifths are shaded in all? [17 fifths] Write this value as the improper fraction $\frac{17}{5}$ so that students can connect the model to the fraction.

6. Provide students with another improper fraction and mixed number. Have them work in pairs to model the numbers and to write a mixed number and an improper fraction based on their models.

Express Improper Fractions and Mixed Numbers in Other Forms

Example 1 Improper Fraction to Mixed Number

You can express improper fractions as mixed numbers.

$\frac{17}{5} = \frac{15}{5} + \frac{2}{5}$ Rewrite as a sum.

$= 3 + \frac{2}{5}$ Write the improper fraction as a whole number.

$= 3\frac{2}{5}$ Write the sum as a mixed number.

Example 2 Mixed Number to Improper Fraction

You can express mixed numbers as improper fractions.

$3\frac{1}{7} = 3 + \frac{1}{7}$ Rewrite as a sum.

$= \frac{21}{7} + \frac{1}{7}$ Write the whole number as a fraction.

$= \frac{22}{7}$ Write the sum as an improper fraction.

✔ Quick Check

Express each improper fraction as a mixed number in simplest form.

1 $\frac{12}{8}$ _____ **2** $\frac{19}{11}$ _____ **3** $\frac{11}{3}$ _____

Express each mixed number as an improper fraction.

4 $4\frac{7}{9}$ _____ **5** $6\frac{2}{7}$ _____ **6** $5\frac{3}{10}$ _____

Practice on Your Own
Express each improper fraction as a mixed number in simplest form.

7 $\frac{12}{9}$ _____ **8** $\frac{24}{5}$ _____ **9** $\frac{11}{7}$ _____

10 $\frac{22}{8}$ _____ **11** $\frac{13}{11}$ _____ **12** $\frac{27}{9}$ _____

13 $\frac{14}{5}$ _____ **14** $\frac{32}{10}$ _____ **15** $\frac{60}{8}$ _____

Express each mixed number as an improper fraction.

16 $2\frac{2}{7}$ _____ **17** $3\frac{4}{9}$ _____ **18** $5\frac{1}{6}$ _____

10 $6\frac{5}{12}$ _____ **20** $1\frac{1}{7}$ _____ **21** $2\frac{8}{9}$ _____

22 $4\frac{2}{9}$ _____ **23** $7\frac{5}{8}$ _____ **24** $8\frac{4}{7}$ _____

Add and Subtract Fractions

TEACHING STRATEGY

1. **Vocabulary** Review the term *common denominator* with students. **Ask** If two fractions have unlike denominators, how can you find a common denominator? [Find the product of the two denominators.] After you identify the common denominator, how do you rewrite each fraction? [Multiply both the numerator and denominator of each fraction by the denominator of the other fraction.]

2. **Teach** Work through both examples with students. In Example 1, make sure students understand that because they get an improper fraction in the sum, they must write it as a mixed number and simplify. **Ask** How do you know that $\frac{19}{15}$ is an improper fraction? [The numerator is greater than the denominator.] When subtracting mixed numbers, what should you do if the numerator in the first fraction is less than the numerator in the second fraction? [Regroup the first mixed number. Subtract 1 from the whole number, then add that 1 to the fraction so that it becomes an improper fraction.]

3. **Quick Check** Look for these common errors as students solve the Quick Check exercises.
   - Forgetting to simplify the answer.
   - Subtracting the fraction part from the whole number part in a mixed number as the final step when subtracting fractions.

4. **Next Steps** Assign the practice exercises to students who show understanding. For students who need more support, provide tutoring using the alternate teaching strategy.

Additional Teaching Resource
🖱 Online Transition Guide with Reteach and Extra Practice worksheets from previous grade levels

ALTERNATE INTERVENTION STRATEGY

Materials: none

Strategy: Use models to add fractions with unlike denominators.

1. Write $\frac{1}{2} + \frac{1}{3}$ on the board.

2. Draw a model for each fraction but do not shade them. **Ask** How many sections of the first model do you shade to show $\frac{1}{2}$? [1 section] How many sections of the first model do you shade to show $\frac{1}{3}$? [1 section]

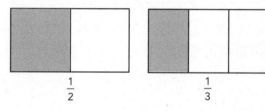

$$\frac{1}{2} \qquad \frac{1}{3}$$

3. Explain to students that the first step in adding fractions with unlike denominators is to rewrite both fractions with a common denominator. **Ask** What is the LCD of 2 and 3? [6] Work with students to rewrite $\frac{1}{2}$ as $\frac{3}{6}$ and $\frac{1}{3}$ as $\frac{2}{6}$.

4. Subdivide each model so that each one is divided into sixths. **Ask** How can you tell that that $\frac{3}{6}$ is equivalent to $\frac{1}{2}$? [In each model, the same amount of the whole is shaded.]

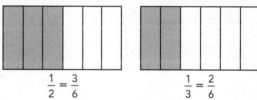

$$\frac{1}{2} = \frac{3}{6} \qquad \frac{1}{3} = \frac{2}{6}$$

5. Have students use the models to find the sum. **Ask** How many shaded parts are there in all? [5] How many parts is each model divided into? [6] Write $\frac{1}{2} + \frac{1}{3} = \frac{3}{6} + \frac{2}{6} = \frac{5}{6}$ on the board.

Add and Subtract Fractions

Name _____ Date _____

Example 1 | Add Fractions

Add $3\frac{2}{3} + 4\frac{3}{5}$.

$= 3 + \frac{2}{3} + 4 + \frac{3}{5}$ Rewrite the sum.

$= 7 + \frac{2 \cdot 5}{3 \cdot 5} + \frac{3 \cdot 3}{5 \cdot 3}$ Rewrite the fractions with a common denominator.

$= 7 + \frac{10}{15} + \frac{9}{15}$ Simplify.

$= 7 + \frac{19}{15}$ Add the fractions.

$= 7 + 1\frac{4}{15}$ Write the improper fraction as a mixed number.

$= 8\frac{4}{15}$ Simplify.

Example 2 | Subtract Fractions

Subtract $5\frac{1}{3} - 3\frac{2}{7}$.

$= \left(5 + \frac{1}{3}\right) - \left(3 + \frac{2}{7}\right)$ Rewrite the difference.

$= (5 - 3) + \left(\frac{1}{3} - \frac{2}{7}\right)$ Subtract

$= 2 + \left(\frac{1}{3} - \frac{2}{7}\right)$ Simplify.

$= 2 + \left(\frac{1 \cdot 7}{3 \cdot 7} - \frac{2 \cdot 3}{7 \cdot 3}\right)$ Rewrite the fractions with a common denominator.

$= 2 + \left(\frac{7}{21} - \frac{6}{21}\right)$ Simplify.

$= 2 + \frac{1}{21}$ Subtract.

$= 2\frac{1}{21}$ Write the whole number and fraction as a mixed number.

✔ Quick Check

Add or subtract. Express your answer in simplest form.

1 $3\frac{1}{4} + 4\frac{3}{5}$

2 $5\frac{2}{3} - 1\frac{5}{9}$

3 $\frac{4}{5} - \frac{3}{7}$

_____   _____   _____

Practice on Your Own
Add or subtract. Express your answer in simplest form.

4 $7\frac{3}{4} - 3\frac{2}{7}$

5 $6\frac{3}{8} + 2\frac{2}{9}$

6 $9\frac{6}{8} - 2\frac{2}{5}$

_____   _____   _____

7 $6\frac{3}{7} + 1\frac{2}{5}$

8 $1\frac{5}{9} - \frac{1}{4}$

9 $4\frac{3}{5} + 1\frac{1}{2}$

_____   _____   _____

Multiply Fractions

| TEACHING STRATEGY | ALTERNATE INTERVENTION STRATEGY |

TEACHING STRATEGY

1. **Vocabulary** Make sure students understand the terms *numerator* and *denominator*. Have volunteers identify an example of each in the first example.

2. **Teach** Review the steps for multiplying fractions. Point out that it is a good idea to write fraction multiplication problems horizontally in order to keep the numerators and denominators lined up. Remind students that simplifying a fraction means there are no common factors in the numerator and denominator. **Ask** In the first example, how do you know that the final product needs to be simplified? [15 and 30 have common factors: 1, 3, 5, and 15. So it is not in simplest form.] Direct students to Example 2. **Ask** In this method, why don't you need to simply the product as the last step? [You have already reduced the fractions to lower terms in the first and second steps, so you do not need to simplify the product as a final step.]

3. **Quick Check** Look for these common errors as students solve the Quick Check exercises.
   - Incorrectly writing the product of the numerators over one of the denominators instead of over the product of the denominators.
   - Mistakenly adding both numerators and both denominators instead of finding their products.

4. **Next Steps** Assign the practice exercises to students who show understanding. For students who need more support, provide tutoring using the alternate teaching strategy.

Additional Teaching Resource

🖱 Online Transition Guide with Reteach and Extra Practice worksheets from previous grade levels

ALTERNATE INTERVENTION STRATEGY

Materials: colored pencils; Optional: TRT14 (Centimeter Grid Paper)

Strategy: Use rectangular arrays to model multiplication of fractions.

1. Write $\frac{2}{3} \cdot \frac{4}{7}$ on the board.

2. Have students draw a rectangle and divide it into 3 equal rows. (You may want to have them use grid paper.) Explain that each row represents one-third. Have students shade 2 of the 3 rows to represent two-thirds.

3. Next instruct students to divide the rectangle into 7 columns of equal width. **Ask** Why are we dividing the rectangle into 7 columns? [to represent sevenths] To represent $\frac{4}{7}$, how many columns should you shade? [4] Have students use a second color to shade 4 columns.

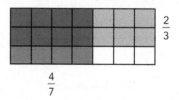

4. Explain to students that they have now modeled the product of $\frac{2}{3} \cdot \frac{4}{7}$. **Ask** How many squares are shaded both colors? [8] How many squares are there in the model in all? [21] On the board, write $\frac{2}{3} \cdot \frac{4}{7} = \frac{8}{21}$.

5. Have students work in pairs to model $\frac{4}{5} \cdot \frac{3}{4} = \frac{3}{5}$.

Name _____ Date _____

Multiply Fractions

Example 1 | **Method 1** _____

Find $\frac{3}{5} \cdot \frac{5}{6}$.

$= \frac{3 \cdot 5}{5 \cdot 6}$ Multiply the numerators.
Multiply the denominators.

$= \frac{15}{30}$ Find the products.

$= \frac{15 \div 15}{30 \div 15} = \frac{1}{2}$ Simplify.

Example 2 | **Method 2** _____

Find $\frac{3}{5} \cdot \frac{5}{6}$.

$= \frac{3}{{}^{1}\cancel{5}} \cdot \frac{\cancel{5}^{1}}{6}$ Divide a numerator and
denominator by the
common factor 5.

$= \frac{{}^{1}\cancel{3}}{1} \cdot \frac{1}{\cancel{6}_{2}}$ Divide the other numerator
and denominator by the
common factor 3.

$= \frac{1 \cdot 1}{1 \cdot 2} = \frac{1}{2}$ Multiply the numerators.
Multiply the denominators.

✔ Quick Check

Multiply. Express your answer in simplest form.

1 $\frac{4}{5} \cdot \frac{3}{4}$

2 $\frac{4}{9} \cdot \frac{5}{6}$

3 $\frac{3}{8} \cdot \frac{1}{6}$

_____   _____   _____

Practice on Your Own
Multiply. Express your answer in simplest form.

4 $\frac{4}{7} \cdot \frac{7}{12}$

5 $\frac{2}{9} \cdot \frac{3}{14}$

6 $\frac{12}{15} \cdot \frac{5}{6}$

_____   _____   _____

7 $\frac{3}{10} \cdot \frac{2}{10}$

8 $\frac{4}{5} \cdot \frac{3}{8}$

9 $\frac{2}{3} \cdot \frac{8}{9}$

_____   _____   _____

10 $\frac{7}{10} \cdot \frac{6}{11}$

11 $\frac{4}{8} \cdot \frac{2}{7}$

12 $\frac{5}{8} \cdot \frac{5}{10}$

_____   _____   _____

Divide Fractions

TEACHING STRATEGY	ALTERNATE INTERVENTION STRATEGY

TEACHING STRATEGY

1. **Vocabulary** Make sure students understand the term *reciprocal*. Have volunteers name the reciprocal of $\frac{3}{4}$. $\left[\frac{4}{3}\right]$

2. **Teach** Work through both examples with students. Before beginning Example 1, explain that dividing by a number yields the same result as multiplying by its reciprocal. Have students look at the first example. **Ask** Which fraction is the divisor? $\left[\frac{5}{8}\right]$ How do you write the reciprocal of a fraction? [Reverse its numerator and denominator.] What is the reciprocal of $\frac{5}{8}$? $\left[\frac{5}{8}\right]$ Review the second example with students, contrasting its steps with the first method. Have students compare the processes of multiplying and dividing fractions. [Possible answer: After you have rewritten a division expression as a multiplication expression by with the reciprocal of the divisor, the process is the same.]

3. **Quick Check** Look for these common errors as students solve the Quick Check exercises.
   - Forgetting to rewrite the problem using the reciprocal of the divisor before multiplying the terms.
   - Mistakenly rewriting the problem using reciprocals for both the divisor and the dividend.

4. **Next Steps** Assign the practice exercises to students who show understanding. For students who need more support, provide tutoring using the alternate teaching strategy.

Additional Teaching Resource

 Online Transition Guide with Reteach and Extra Practice worksheets from previous grade levels

ALTERNATE INTERVENTION STRATEGY

Materials: none

Strategy: Use models to divide fractions.

1. Write $\frac{1}{2} \div \frac{1}{4}$ on the board.

2. Explain to students that the problem is asking you to divide $\frac{1}{2}$ into quarters, or to find how many quarters there are in $\frac{1}{2}$. Draw a model for $\frac{1}{2}$ on the board.

3. Explain to students that you need to divide this model into fourths. **Ask** Why do we need to divide this model into fourths? [Because you are dividing by $\frac{1}{4}$.] Draw the model divided into fourths on the board.

4. Have students examine the model. **Ask** How many shaded pieces of fourths are there? [2] On the board, write $\frac{1}{2} \div \frac{1}{4} = 2$.

5. Have students work in pairs to model $\frac{1}{4} \div \frac{1}{2} = \frac{1}{2}$.

Divide Fractions

Example 1 Method 1

Find $\dfrac{7}{12} \cdot \dfrac{5}{8}$.

$= \dfrac{7}{12} \cdot \dfrac{5}{8}$ Replace the divisor with its reciprocal, and rewrite as a multiplication expression.

$= \dfrac{7 \cdot 8}{12 \cdot 5}$ Multiply the numerators. Multiply the denominators.

$= \dfrac{56}{60}$ Find the products.

$= \dfrac{56 \div 4}{60 \div 4} = \dfrac{14}{15}$ Simplify.

Example 2 Method 2

Find $\dfrac{7}{12} \div \dfrac{5}{8}$.

$= \dfrac{7}{12} \cdot \dfrac{5}{8}$ Replace the divisor with its reciprocal, and rewrite as a multiplication expression.

$= \dfrac{7}{_3\cancel{12}} \cdot \dfrac{\cancel{8}^2}{5}$ Divide a numerator and denominator by the common factor 4.

$= \dfrac{7 \cdot 2}{3 \cdot 5} = \dfrac{14}{15}$ Find the products.

✔ Quick Check
Divide. Express your answer in simplest form.

1 $\dfrac{2}{3} \div \dfrac{8}{9}$

2 $\dfrac{3}{8} \div \dfrac{3}{4}$

3 $\dfrac{3}{7} \cdot \dfrac{1}{6}$

_____

_____

_____

Practice on Your Own
Divide. Express your answer in simplest form.

4 $\dfrac{4}{7} \div \dfrac{5}{14}$

5 $\dfrac{2}{21} \div \dfrac{6}{7}$

6 $\dfrac{3}{4} \div \dfrac{9}{10}$

_____

_____

_____

7 $\dfrac{9}{10} \div \dfrac{3}{5}$

8 $\dfrac{3}{10} \div \dfrac{5}{6}$

9 $\dfrac{4}{7} \div \dfrac{2}{5}$

_____

_____

_____

10 $\dfrac{4}{5} \div \dfrac{3}{4}$

11 $\dfrac{3}{5} \div \dfrac{2}{7}$

12 $\dfrac{5}{12} \div \dfrac{3}{10}$

_____

_____

_____

Multiply Decimals

TEACHING STRATEGY

1. **Vocabulary** Remind students that a product is the result of multiplying two or more numbers (factors).

2. **Teach** Explain to students that multiplying decimals works just like multiplying whole numbers. The only difference is placing the decimal point as a last step. **Ask** If you multiply 2.55 by 13.3, how many decimal places will be in the product? Explain. [3; the sum of the 2 decimal places in the first factor and the 1 decimal place in the second factor] Review Example 1. **Ask** Why is the product 97.98 and not 9,798? [Each factor has 1 decimal place so the product must have 2 decimal places.] Then direct students' attention to Example 2. **Ask** Look at the factors. How many decimal places will be in the product? Explain. [There will be 3 decimal places in the product because there are 2 decimal places in the first factor and 1 place in the second factor.]

3. **Quick Check** Look for these common errors as students solve the Quick Check exercises.
   • Misplacing the decimal point in the product.
   • Forgetting to place the decimal point in the product.
   • Making computation errors by incorrectly lining up the factors on their decimal points before multiplying.

4. **Next Steps** Assign the practice exercises to students who show understanding. For students who need more support, provide tutoring using the alternate teaching strategy.

Additional Teaching Resource

 Online Transition Guide with Reteach and Extra Practice worksheets from previous grade levels

ALTERNATE INTERVENTION STRATEGY

Materials: TRT4 (Hundredths Grids), colored pencils

Strategy: Use models to multiply decimals.

1. Write the multiplication problem 0.5 · 0.3 on the board.

2. Distribute hundredths grids to students. **Ask** How many columns do we need to shade to show 0.5? [5] Shade the first 5 columns of the hundreds grid. **Ask** How many rows do we need to shade to show 0.3? [3] Shade the bottom 3 rows of the hundreds grid in a different color. Explain that the product is the section shaded in both colors. **Ask** How many squares in the grid are shaded both colors? [15] What is 15 hundredths written as a decimal? [0.15]

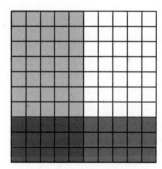

3. Repeat the process for the problem 2 · 0.3. Have students shade 3 columns in a hundreds grid in one color and then shade another 3 columns in a second color to double the value. **Ask** How many columns are shaded in all? [6] What decimal does the model represent? [0.6]

4. Write 0.5 · 0.3 = 0.15 and 2 · 0.3 = 0.6 on the board. Have students compare the factors and products. **Ask** What decimal pattern do you notice about the factors and their products? [The total number of decimal places in the factors is the same as the decimal places in the products.]

Multiply Decimals

Name _____ Date _____

Example 1

First multiply. Then count the number of decimal places in the original numbers. Place the decimal point so that the product has the same number of decimal places.

$$42.6 \leftarrow 1 \text{ decimal place}$$
$$\times \ \ 2.3 \leftarrow + 1 \text{ decimal place}$$
$$1278$$
$$+ 8520$$
$$\overline{97.98} \leftarrow 2 \text{ decimal places}$$

Example 2

Find $5.15 \cdot 3.7$.

First multiply. Then place the decimal point.

$$5.15 \leftarrow 2 \text{ decimal places}$$
$$\times \ \ 3.7 \leftarrow + 1 \text{ decimal place}$$
$$3605$$
$$+ 15450$$
$$\overline{19.055} \leftarrow 3 \text{ decimal places}$$

✔ Quick Check

Multiply. Express your answer in its simplest form.

1 $6.4 \cdot 11.3$

2 $8.3 \cdot 10.1$

3 $4.52 \cdot 2.9$

Practice on Your Own
Multiply. Express your answer in its simplest form.

4 $12.33 \cdot 2.1$

5 $3.5 \cdot 8.02$

6 $15.4 \cdot 2.7$

7 $9.6 \cdot 0.75$

8 $13.63 \cdot 5.6$

9 $7.8 \cdot 3.9$

10 $6.05 \cdot 7.2$

11 $12.98 \cdot 6.4$

12 $34 \cdot 5.6$

13 $15.4 \cdot 0.17$

14 $18.92 \cdot 0.1$

15 $8.5 \cdot 10.5$

Divide Decimals

TEACHING STRATEGY

1. **Vocabulary** Review the terms in a division problem: *dividend*, *divisor*, and *quotient*. Explain that, when written horizontally, the dividend is the first term, the divisor is the second term, and the quotient is the result.

2. **Teach** Work through the examples with students. **Ask** Why do you multiply the denominator by a power of 10 in the second step? [It makes it easier to do the division because the divisor is a whole number.] Explain to students that by multiplying by a power of 10, they are, in effect, moving the decimal the same number of places in the divisor and the dividend. Finally, write $9.45 \div 2.1 = 4.5$ and $1.68 \div 0.3 = 5.6$ on the board. Ask students to compare the dividends, divisors, and quotients. **Ask** What pattern do you see in the relationship between the quotients, divisors, and dividends in each problem? [When the divisor is greater than 1, the quotient will be less than the dividend. When the divisor is less than 1, the quotient is larger than the dividend.]

3. **Quick Check** Look for these common errors as students solve the Quick Check exercises.
   • Forgetting to place the decimal point in the quotient.
   • Neglecting to multiply both the numerator and the denominator by the same power of 10.

4. **Next Steps** Assign the practice exercises to students who show understanding. For students who need more support, provide tutoring using the alternate teaching strategy.

Additional Teaching Resource
Online Transition Guide with Reteach and Extra Practice worksheets from previous grade levels

ALTERNATE INTERVENTION STRATEGY

Materials: TRT4 (Hundredths Grids), scissors

Strategy: Use models to divide decimals

1. Write the division problem $1.8 \div 0.6$ on the board.

2. Model 1.8 by shading and cutting out one block of 10 tenths and 8 tenths to represent 1.8.

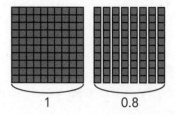

1   0.8

3. Cut the blocks into individual tenths strips. Explain to students that you do this because you are dividing by 6 tenths. **Ask** How many tenths are there? [18]

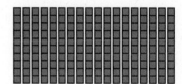

4. Divide the strips into equal groups of 6 tenths to model dividing by 0.6. **Ask** How many equal groups of 6 tenths can be formed from 1.8? [3] Write the number sentence $1.8 \div 0.6 = 3$ on the board.

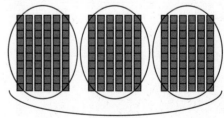

3 groups

5. Write the problem $2.8 \div 0.4$ on the board. Have students work in pairs to model the problem and record the quotient.

Divide Decimals

Example 1

Find $14.5 \div 2.5$.

$14.5 \div 2.5 = \dfrac{14.5}{2.5}$ Rewrite division as a fraction.

$= \dfrac{14.5}{2.5} \cdot \dfrac{10}{10}$ Make the denominator a whole number by multiplying it by a power of 10. Multiply the numerator too.

$= \dfrac{145}{25}$ Simplify the fraction.

$= 5.8$ Divide as you would with whole numbers.

Example 2

Find $31.71 \div 3.02$.

$31.71 \div 3.02 = \dfrac{31.71}{3.02}$ Rewrite division as a fraction.

$= \dfrac{31.71}{3.02} \cdot \dfrac{100}{100}$ Make the denominator a whole number by multiplying it by a power of 10. Multiply the numerator too.

$= \dfrac{3,171}{302}$ Simplify the fraction.

$= 5.8$ Divide as you would with whole numbers.

✔ Quick Check

Divide. Express your answer in its simplest form.

1 $36.45 \div 8.1$ **2** $91.14 \div 2.17$ **3** $9.225 \div 0.75$

_____   _____   _____

Practice on Your Own

Divide. Express your answer in its simplest form.

4 $2.31 \div 0.15$ **5** $38.54 \div 8.2$ **6** $15.4 \div 2.75$

_____   _____   _____

7 $3.6 \div 0.75$ **8** $22.54 \div 2.45$ **9** $7.98 \div 0.6$

_____   _____   _____

10 $0.205 \div 4.1$ **11** $12.98 \div 4.4$ **12** $34.83 \div 8.6$

_____   _____   _____

13 $9.1 \div 2.8$ **14** $46.92 \div 5.1$ **15** $18.96 \div 0.8$

_____   _____   _____

Use Percents

TEACHING STRATEGY

1. **Vocabulary** Make sure students understand the term *percent*. Explain that the word percent means "per hundred." A percent is a comparison, or ratio, of a quantity to 100. Ask volunteers to share examples of using percents in their daily lives.

2. **Teach** Work through the Example 1 with students. **Ask** Why do you write 60% as $\frac{60}{100}$ in the first step? [A percent is a comparison of a number to 100, so you can write 60% as a ratio of 60 to 100 in fraction form.] How can you check the answer? [Divide 75 by 125 and multiply the quotient by 100%. The answer is 60%.] How much does Jamie pay? [$125 – $75 = $50] Have students look at Example 2. **Ask** Why do you write the ratio as $\frac{45}{90}$ in the second step? [You are being asked to find the percent increase in the amount of snow. So you need to compare the increase in the amount of snow to the amount of snow last year.] How can you check the answer? [You can find 50% of 90. The answer is 45.]

3. **Quick Check** Look for these common errors as students solve the Quick Check exercises.
   - Confusing the order of the terms in a ratio when calculating what percent one quantity is of another quantity.
   - Forgetting to multiply by 100% when calculating percent.

4. **Next Steps** Assign the practice exercises to students who show understanding. For students who need more support, provide tutoring using the alternate teaching strategy.

> **Additional Teaching Resource**
> Online Transition Guide with Reteach and Extra Practice worksheets from previous grade levels

ALTERNATE INTERVENTION STRATEGY

Materials: none

Strategy: Use bar models to solve percent problems.

1. Tell students that they will be using a bar model to help them visualize a percent problem.

2. Write the following problem on the board: In a school, 129 out of 430 students play in an extracurricular sport. What percent of students play in an extracurricular sport?

3. Draw a bar model to represent the problem. Explain to students the model shows that 430 is 100% of the students. They need to find what percent represents 129 students. **Ask** If you know that 430 is 100% of the students, how can you figure out what 1% of the students is? [You can divide 430 by 100; 430 ÷ 100 = 4.3] Explain that you can find the percent by calculating how many times 4.3 goes into 129: 129 ÷ 4.3 = 30, so 30% of the students play in an extracurricular sport.

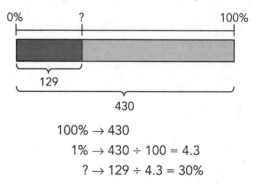

$$100\% \rightarrow 430$$
$$1\% \rightarrow 430 \div 100 = 4.3$$
$$? \rightarrow 129 \div 4.3 = 30\%$$

4. If students need additional help with percent increase and decrease, then share the following problem: Mina biked 48 miles last week but only 12 miles this week. Find the percent decrease in the distance Mina biked. Repeat the process by drawing a bar model to represent the situation and working through the problem with students. [75%]

EE
SKILL 15 # Use Percents

A percent is a ratio or comparison of a quantity to 100.

Example 1 **Find Percent** ──────────

At a going-out-of-business sale, Jamie buys a microwave oven for 60% off. The original cost of the oven is $125. Find the amount that Jamie saves on the cost of the oven.

Write the percent as a fraction.

$60\% = \dfrac{60}{100}$

Multiply by the original cost to solve.

$\dfrac{60}{100} \cdot 125 = \dfrac{7{,}500}{100}$

$= 75$

Jamie saves $75.

Example 2 **Find Percent Change** ──────────

Last winter, a town received 90 cm of snow. This winter, it received 135 cm of snow. Find the increase in the amount of snow. Then find the percent increase in the amount of snow.

$135 - 90 = 45$ cm   Subtract to find the increase in the amount of snow.

$\dfrac{45}{90} \cdot 100\%$
$= 0.5 \cdot 100\%$
$= 50\%$

To find the percent increase, write a fraction with the difference you calculated as the numerator and the original amount of snow as the denominator. Then multiply the quotient by 100% to find the percent.

The percent increase in the amount of snow is 50%.

✔ Quick Check
Solve each percent problem.

1 What is 15% of 80? _____

2 45 is what percent of 125? _____

3 A sports store sells 105 pairs of sneakers in April. In May, the store sells 42 pair of sneakers.

   a) Find the decrease in the number of pairs of sneakers sold from April to May. _____

   b) Find the percent decrease in the number of sneakers sold from April to May. _____

Practice on Your Own
Solve each percent problem.

4 What is 40% of 200? _____

5 33 is what percent of 120? _____

6 What is 70% of $70? _____

7 10 is what percent of 200? _____

8 Kai's dog weighed 4 pounds when he adopted it. The dog now weighs 34 pounds.

   a) Find the increase in the weight of Kai's dog. _____

   b) Find the percent increase in the weight of Kai's dog. _____

EE SKILL 16 — Recognize Parts of an Algebraic Expression

TEACHING STRATEGY

1. **Vocabulary** First, make sure students understand that an algebraic expression is a particular type of *mathematical* expression.

2. **Teach** Direct students to the labeled expression. Point out the three uppercase labels. Explain that an algebraic expression is made up of two main parts—operation symbols and terms—and that the different terms in an expression are separated by the operation symbols (+) or (–). **Ask** How many terms are in this expression? [2] What are the two types of terms? [algebraic and numerical] What is the difference between an algebraic term and a numerical term? [An algebraic term must contain at least one variable.] Go on to explain the difference between a number that is a constant and one that is a coefficient.

3. **Quick Check** Look for these common errors as students solve the Quick Check exercises.
   - Misidentifying algebraic terms as numerical terms because they include numbers.
   - Incorrectly identifying a coefficient as a constant term due to lack of understanding that a coefficient is a number that appears *within* an algebraic term and is multiplied by a variable.
   - Misidentifying the number of terms due to a misconception that each number or variable within an expression is a term.

4. **Next Steps** Assign the practice exercises to students who show understanding. For students who need more support, provide tutoring using the alternate teaching strategy.

Additional Teaching Resource
Online Transition Guide with Reteach and Extra Practice worksheets from previous grade levels

ALTERNATE INTERVENTION STRATEGY

Materials: highlighters or colored pencils

Strategy: Use shapes and colors to label the parts of an algebraic expression.

1. Labeling a longer expression can help students better understand its structure. Write 3x + 4 + 6x + 1. Have students copy it.

2. Use shapes to focus first on the top level of hierarchy. Ask a volunteer to circle the (+) and (–) operation symbols. Explain that the terms in an algebraic expression are separated by these symbols. Next, ask a volunteer to draw a rectangle around each term.

$$\boxed{3x} \oplus \boxed{4} \oplus \boxed{6x} \oplus \boxed{1}$$

3. Tell students that there are two types of terms: numerical and algebraic. Explain that a numerical term includes only numbers. Ask students to label the numerical terms. Explain that an algebraic term includes at least one variable. Ask students to label the algebraic terms.

4. Use color to explore the next level of hierarchy. Tell students that terms are made up of smaller parts. Explain that numerical terms contain only numbers. Algebraic terms contain variables and may contain numbers.

5. Choose a color for variables. Have a volunteer use that color to highlight the variables in the expression. Explain that a number that is multiplied by a variable in an algebraic term is called a *coefficient*. Choose a second color for coefficients. Have a volunteer use that color to highlight the coefficients in the expression.

6. Work through other examples with students, including expressions that feature negative signs and unseen coefficients of 1. As students become familiar with the parts, phase out the use of shapes and color.

Recognize Parts of an Algebraic Expression

Example

An **algebraic expression**, such as 3y + 5, is a mathematical phrase that contains at least one variable, and may include numbers and operation symbols.

A **variable** is a letter or symbol used to represent an unknown value or quantity. Variables such as x or y represent values that can vary, or change.

A **constant** is a quantity that does not change. A constant is usually a **numerical term** such as 1, 8, –2, $\frac{1}{2}$, or 3.5.

An **operation symbol** represents a mathematical operation such as addition (+), subtraction (–), multiplication (× or ·), or division (÷). **Terms** in an expression are separated by (+) or (–) symbols.

An **algebraic term** includes at least one variable. A **coefficient** is a number multiplied by the variable(s) in an algebraic term.

```
                    OPERATION SYMBOL
        variable         ↓
coefficient →  3y + 5  ← constant
        ALGEBRAIC TERM  NUMERICAL TERM
```

☑ Quick Check

Use the algebraic expression 7 + 5m. Answer the following questions.

1 What is the variable? _____

2 What is the coefficient? _____

3 What is the numerical term? _____

4 How many terms are there? _____

5 What is the operation symbol? _____

Practice on Your Own
In the algebraic expression 6z + (–8), identify the following.

6 the variable _____

7 the coefficient _____

8 the numerical term _____

9 the operation symbol _____

10 the algebraic term _____

11 the constant term _____

12 the number of terms in the expression _____

Evaluate Algebraic Expressions

TEACHING STRATEGY

1. **Vocabulary** Explain that an *algebraic expression* is similar to a *numerical expression*, but an algebraic expression contains at least one variable. Make sure students understand the terms *substitute* and *evaluate*. Explain that to substitute a value into an expression is to replace a variable with a given value (a number). Evaluating an expression means to substitute a given value for the variable and then simplify the expression.

2. **Teach** Review the order of operations with students and point out that they will need to follow the rules to correctly evaluate expressions. Direct students to Example 1. **Ask** What two operations will be used to evaluate this expression? [multiplication then subtraction] **Ask** What number replaces *x*? [3] Work through the example. Point out what happens when you do not follow the correct order of operations. If you subtract before multiplying, 4 · 3 – 5 results in 4 · (–2) = –8, which is an incorrect answer.

3. **Quick Check** Look for these common errors as students solve the Quick Check exercises.
   - Adding or subtracting before multiplying or dividing, indicating unfamiliarity with the correct order of operations.
   - Multiplying when x appears, indicating confusion between the variable x and the multiplication symbol ×.

4. **Next Steps** Assign the practice exercises to students who show understanding. For students who need more support, provide tutoring using the alternate teaching strategy.

Additional Teaching Resource
 Online Transition Guide with Reteach and Extra Practice worksheets from previous grade levels

ALTERNATE INTERVENTION STRATEGY

Materials: TRT2 (Number Cards); TRT3 (Symbol Cards), scissors

Strategy: Represent expressions using cards to physically model substitution.

1. Give students two copies of the number and symbol cards to cut out. Tell them to write the variables *a*, *b*, or *c* on the blank cards.

2. Write the expression 3*a* – 4 on the board and have students model it with cards.

3. **Ask** What does the term 3*a* mean? [The variable a is multiplied by 3.] On the board, write 3 · *a* – 4. Have students revise their models.

4. Write *a* = 5 on the board. Tell students that to evaluate the expression when *a* = 5, they must substitute. **Ask** How do we substitute 5 for the variable *a*? [Replace the *a* in the expression with 5.] On the board, write 3 · 5 – 4. Have students revise their models.

5. **Ask** What operations do you see? [multiplication and subtraction] According to the order of operations, which of those do you do first? [multiplication] What is the product 3 · 5? [15] On the board, write 15 – 4. Have students revise their models.

6. What is the difference 15 – 4? [11] On the board, write 11. Have students revise their models.

7. Repeat the process with several other expressions. When students understand how to substitute and evaluate expressions using the models, have them evaluate expressions with paper and pencil.

Name _____ Date _____

Evaluate Algebraic Expressions

Example 1

Given that $x = 3$ in the expression $4x - 5$, find the value of the expression.

STEP 1 Substitute. Replace the variable x in the expression with the value 3.
$$4x - 5 = 4 \cdot 3 - 5$$

STEP 2 According to the order of operations, multiply before subtracting.
$$4 \cdot 3 - 5 = 12 - 5$$

STEP 3 Subtract.
$$12 - 5 = 7$$

Example 2

Given that $d = -2$ in the expression $-4d + 6$, find the value of the expression.

STEP 1 Substitute. Replace the variable d in the expression with the value -2.
$$-4d + 6 = (-4) \cdot (-2) + 6$$

STEP 1 According to the order of operations, multiply before adding.
$$(-4) \cdot (-2) + 6 = 8 + 6$$

STEP 1 Add.
$$8 + 6 = 14$$

☑ Quick Check

Evaluate each expression for the given value of the variable.

1 $15 - 2a$ when $a = 3$

_____

2 $7b + 3$ when $b = 2$

_____

3 $3c + 5$ when $c = 0$

_____

4 $\dfrac{t}{2} - 3$ when $t = 16$

_____

5 $-r + 7$ when $r = 5$

_____

6 $-3x - 6$ when $x = -4$

_____

Practice on Your Own
Complete the table.

y	$y - 4$	$5y$	$3y + 2$
3	$3 - 4 = -1$		
0			
−2			
5			
−4			

EE
SKILL 18
Simplify Algebraic Expressions

TEACHING STRATEGY

1. **Vocabulary** Remind students that a variable is a letter that represents an unknown value, a value that can change. Explain that a *coefficient* is the number that is multiplied by the variable in an algebraic term. Also remind students that a term that contains only a number is called a *constant*. A term that contains only a variable is understood to have a coefficient of 1.

2. **Teach** Direct students to Example 1. **Ask** Why are 7x and 2x like terms? [because they include the same variable, *x*] What is the coefficient in the term 7x? [7] How do we combine the terms 7x and 2x? [Find the sum of their coefficients: 7 + 2 = 9, so 7x + 2x = 9x.] Direct students to Example 2. **Ask** How many terms does the expression contain? [4] Which terms can be combined? [2a and a; 6 and −11] Why? [because they are pairs of like terms] In the term *a*, what is the coefficient? [1]

3. **Quick Check** Look for these common errors as students solve the Quick Check exercises.
   - Forgetting that when a variable stands alone in an algebraic expression, it is understood to have a coefficient of 1.
   - Incorrectly combining like and unlike terms.
   - Computation errors that indicate a lack of proficiency with addition and subtraction of positive and negative numbers.

4. **Next Steps** Assign the practice exercises to students who show understanding. For students who need more support, provide tutoring using the alternate teaching strategy.

Additional Teaching Resource

Online Transition Guide with Reteach and Extra Practice worksheets from previous grade levels

ALTERNATE INTERVENTION STRATEGY

Materials: none

Strategy: Use shapes to help identify and combine like terms.

1. Remind students that like terms must have identical variables. Write the expression 12x + 1 + 7x + 19 on the board.

2. Circle each constant term and draw a rectangle around each x-term.

$$\boxed{12x} + ⃝1 + \boxed{7x} + ⃝{19}$$

3. Discuss like terms. **Ask** Can you add circles and rectangles and get a common term? [No] Can you add constants and variables and get a common term? [No] What is the sum of the terms in rectangles? [19x] What is the sum of the terms in circles? [20] What is the simplified form of the expression? [19x + 20]

4. Write the expression 7n − 6 − 3n + 10 on the board.

5. Have one volunteer draw a circle around each constant term, and another volunteer draw a rectangle around each n-term. Remind them both to include the negative signs.

$$\boxed{7n} \;⃝{-6}\; \boxed{-n} + ⃝{10}$$

6. **Ask** What is the coefficient of the third term? [−1] Then instruct students to simplify the expression. Emphasize that they should be careful with negatives. [6n + 4].

7. Have students simplify a number of expressions using this technique. As they become proficient at recognizing and combining like terms, phase out the use of circles and rectangles.

Simplify Algebraic Expressions

Example 1

Simplify the expression.

$7x - 2 + 2x$

Reorder terms: $7x + 2x - 2$

Add like (x) terms: $7x + 2x = (7 + 2)x =$ **$9x$**

Keep term: **-2** (also keep the minus sign)

The simplified expression is $9x - 2$.

Example 2

Simplify the expression.

$$2a + 6 + a - 11$$

Reorder terms: $2a + a + 6 - 11$

Add like (a) terms: $2a + a = (2 + 1)a =$ **$3a$**

Add constant terms: $6 - 11 =$ **-5**

The simplified expression is $3a - 5$.

✔ Quick Check

State whether each expression can be simplified. Explain your reasoning.

1 $2x + 4 - 10y$

2 $14b - 2 - 17b$

Simplify each expression.

3 $-5c + c$

4 $-4u - 7 + 3u$

Practice on Your Own
Simplify each expression.

5 $2x + 10x$

6 $22m + 16 - 11m$

7 $8 - 12d + 4d$

8 $16j + 8 - j$

9 $-9y + 4y - 8$

10 $-3 + 6x + 7 + x$

Expand Algebraic Expressions

TEACHING STRATEGY

1. **Vocabulary** Make sure students understand that the distributive property involves multiplication with addition or subtraction. It shows how to multiply one expression by a second expression that has more that one term and is written within parentheses. You "distribute" the first expression to each of the terms within the parentheses.

2. **Teach** Remind students that the distributive property states that $a(b + c) = ab + ac$. Refer to Example 1. **Ask** What is the first step in expanding an algebraic expression? [Multiply each term inside the parentheses by the term outside the parentheses.] Remind students that the expanded form of the expression must use the same sign as in the original expression. Then direct students' attention to Example 2. **Ask** Why is the correct answer $21 + 7h$ and not $28h$? [21 and $7h$ are unlike terms because only one term has a variable. So they cannot be combined.]

3. **Quick Check** Look for these common errors as students solve the Quick Check exercises.
   - Combining unlike terms: $3 + 3y \neq 6y$.
   - Writing the wrong operation sign, perhaps indicating a lack of understanding that the product of a positive factor and a negative factor is negative.
   - Forgetting that 1 is the coefficient of a variable with no visible coefficient.

4. **Next Steps** Assign the practice exercises to students who show understanding. For students who need more support, provide tutoring using the alternate teaching strategy.

Additional Teaching Resource

🖱 Online Transition Guide with Reteach and Extra Practice worksheets from previous grade levels

ALTERNATE INTERVENTION STRATEGY

Materials: TRT14 (Centimeter Grid Paper), scissors

Strategy: Use models to understand the distributive property.

1. Write the expression 4 • 12 on the board.

2. Guide students as they make an array to show 4 • 12. **Ask** How many squares high should the array be? [4 squares] How many squares long? [12 squares] Have students outline the array on the grid paper and cut the array out.

3. Demonstrate how to fold the array to break apart the 12 columns into 10 columns and 2 columns. **Ask** How many tens do you have, left of the fold? [4 • 1 ten = 4 tens or 40] How many ones do you have, right of the fold? [4 • 2 ones = 8 ones or 8] How many do you have in all? [40 + 8 = 48]

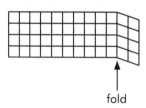

fold

4. Write the following on the board:

$$4 \cdot 12 = 4(10 + 2)$$
$$= 4(10) + 4(2)$$
$$= 40 + 8$$
$$= 48$$

Guide students to see that multiplying a sum by a certain factor is the same as multiplying each addend (10 and 2) by that factor and then adding their products.

5. Proceed in a similar manner with other numerical expressions. When students are able to work without models, have them expand these algebraic expressions:

$3(x + 2)$ and $4(3 - 2y)$.

Expand Algebraic Expressions

Example 1

Expand the expression.

$$5(2d - 4)$$

STEP 1 Apply the distributive property. Multiply by 5 each of the terms $2d$ and 4.

$$5(2d - 4) = 5(2d) - 5(4)$$

STEP 1 Multiply within each term.

$$5(2d) - 5(4) = 10d - 20$$

The expanded form of $5(2d - 4)$ is $10d - 20$.

Example 2

Expand the expression.

$$7(3 + h)$$

STEP 1 Apply the distributive property. Multiply by 7 each of the terms 3 and h.

$$7(3 + h) = 7(3) + 7(h)$$

STEP 1 Multiply within each term.

$$7(3) + 7(h) = 21 + 7h$$

The expanded form of $7(3 + h)$ is $21 + 7h$.

✔ Quick Check
Expand each expression.

1 $3(3y - 2)$

_____

2 $8(1 + 6a)$

_____

3 $4(4e + 5)$

_____

Practice on Your Own
Expand each expression.

4 $6(7s + 3)$

_____

5 $8(2 - r)$

_____

6 $3(8 + 4m)$

_____

7 $5(b - 8)$

_____

8 $9(5d + 7)$

_____

9 $4(10s - 2)$

_____

10 $7(7 + 7g)$

_____

11 $10(2k - 9)$

_____

12 $12(3v - 2)$

_____

13 $9(8 + 4w)$

_____

14 $8(6n - 8)$

_____

15 $11(11p + 5)$

_____

Factor Algebraic Expressions

TEACHING STRATEGY

1. **Vocabulary** Make sure students understand the term *greatest common factor* (GCF). Remind them that factors are multiplied together, a common factor is a factor that expressions have in common, and the greatest common factor is simply the greatest of the common factors.

2. **Teach** Direct students to Example 1. **Ask** What are the factors of $6p$? [1, 2, 3, 6, and p.] What are factors of 15? [1, 3, and 5] What are the common factors? [1 and 3] What is the greatest common factor? [3] **Ask** How can you check the answer to Example 1? [Use the distributive property to expand the answer, then compare to the original expression: $3(2p + 5) = 6p + 15$.] Direct students to Example 2, and explain that an expression can be factored only when the GCF of the terms is not 1. **Ask** Why can't you factor the expression $13 – 5n$? [The factors of 13 are 1 and 13. The factors of 5 are 1, 5, and n. The only common factor is 1.]

3. **Quick Check** Look for these common errors as students solve the Quick Check exercises.
   - Incorrectly listing multiples instead of factors, indicating a misunderstanding of the concept.
   - Listing incorrect factors, showing a lack of proficiency with basic multiplication and division facts.

4. **Next Steps** Assign the practice exercises to students who show understanding. For students who need more support, provide tutoring using the alternate teaching strategy.

Additional Teaching Resource
Online Transition Guide with Reteach and Extra Practice worksheets from previous grade levels

ALTERNATE INTERVENTION STRATEGY

Materials: none

Strategy: Use prime factorization to identify the greatest common factor.

1. Explain to students that they can use prime factorization to find the greatest common factor of two numbers. Work through the process using the expression $18x + 24$.

2. Draw a factor tree for each number and have students copy each step as you guide them through the process.

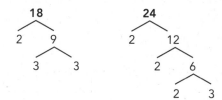

3. Have students write the prime factorization of the two numbers.

   $18 = 2 \times 3 \times 3$

   $24 = 2 \times 2 \times 2 \times 3$

4. Next have students line up matching factors according to occurrence and circle complete pairs.

   $18 = ⃝2 \times \qquad ⃝3 \times 3$
   $24 = ⃝2 \times 2 \times 2 \times ⃝3$

5. Explain that the greatest common factor is the product of the matched pairs only. **Ask** What is the greatest common factor of 18 and 24? [$2 \times 3 = 6$]

6. Show students how to factor the expression using 6 as the common factor: $6(3x + 4)$.

7. Have students work on their own to factor $12y – 27$ using prime factorization. [$3(4y – 9)$]

Factor Algebraic Expressions

Name _____ Date _____

Example 1

Factor the expression.

$$6p + 15$$

STEP 1 Determine the greatest common factor (GCF) of the terms.
The GCF of $6p$ and 15 is 3.

STEP 1 Use the GCF to factor each term.
$6p + 15 = 3(2p) + 3(5)$

STEP 1 Rewrite the expression as a product.
$3(2p) + 3(5) = 3(2p + 5)$

The factored form of $6p + 15$ is $3(2p + 5)$.

Example 2

Factor the expression. If the expression cannot be factored, explain why not.

$$13 - 5n$$

STEP 1 Determine the greatest common factor (GCF) of the terms.
The only common factor of 13 and $5n$ is 1.

STEP 1 Because 1 is the only common factor of 13 and $5n$, you cannot factor the expression $13 - 5n$.

✔ Quick Check

Factor the expression. If the expression cannot be factored, explain why not.

1 $4y + 12$

2 $9 + 5b$

3 $16t - 2$

_____   _____   _____

Practice on Your Own

Factor the expression. If the expression cannot be factored, explain why not.

4 $8j + 18$

5 $12s - 28$

6 $30 + 7h$

_____   _____   _____

7 $3 - 15g$

8 $3 + 14v$

9 $10c + 25$

_____   _____   _____

10 $21x - 14$

11 $10r + 15$

12 $17 + 4f$

_____   _____   _____

Recognize Equivalent Expressions

TEACHING STRATEGY

1. **Vocabulary** Make sure students understand *the term* equivalent. Remind them that the term means "having the same value." Two algebraic expressions are equivalent when they are equal for all values of the variable.

2. **Teach** Explain to students that they can use either the distributive property or factoring to determine if two expressions are equivalent. Have students look at Example 1. **Ask** Why must you first use the distributive property to expand the first expression? [In order to compare the expressions, they have to be in the same form. Since the second expression is already expanded, you can expand the first expression to compare both of them.] How do you know that the expressions are equivalent? [The expanded form of the first expression is the same as the second expression. So they are equal for all values of *g*.] Point out Example 2. **Ask** Why are the two expressions not equivalent? [5(5 + 4*t*) is not the same as 5(6 + 4*t*), so the expressions are not equal for all values of *t*.] Remind students that ≠ is read as "*not equal to.*"

3. **Quick Check** Look for these common errors as students solve the Quick Check exercises.
   • Writing the wrong operation sign when expanding or factoring an expression.
   • Making computation errors when expanding or factoring an expression.

4. **Next Steps** Assign the practice exercises to students who show understanding. For students who need more support, provide tutoring using the alternate teaching strategy.

Additional Teaching Resource
Online Transition Guide with Reteach and Extra Practice worksheets from previous grade levels

ALTERNATE INTERVENTION STRATEGY

Materials: algebra tiles or TRT6 (Algebra Tiles)

Strategy: Use models to recognize equivalent expressions.

1. Write the expression $x + 2$ on the board. Have students use algebra tiles to model $x + 2$. On the board, below the expression $x + 2$, draw the model.

2. Write the expression $3(x + 2)$ on the board. **Ask** How do we change our model of $x + 2$ so that it shows $3(x + 2)$? [Repeat the model of $x + 2$ two more times, so that it appears a total of 3 times.] Have students use tiles to model $3(x + 2)$. On the board, below the expression $3(x + 2)$, draw the model.

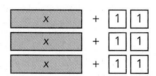

3. **Ask** How many x tiles are there in all? [3] What algebraic term represents the x tiles? [3x] How many 1 tiles are there in all? [6] On the board, below the model, write the expression $3x + 6$.

4. Explain to students that $3(x + 2)$ and $3x + 6$ are equivalent expressions because the same model can be used to represent both expressions.

5. Repeat this process with $2(3x + 4)$. Once students are comfortable with using the tiles to model expressions, have them determine if $4(2x + 5)$ and $8x + 20$ are equivalent expressions without the use of algebra tiles.

EE
SKILL 21

Recognize Equivalent Expressions

Example 1 Through Expanding	**Example 2** Through Factoring
Determine whether the algebraic expressions below are equivalent. $3(2g - 4)$ and $6g - 12$	Determine whether the algebraic expressions below are equivalent. $25 + 20t$ and $5(6 + 4t)$
STEP 1 Use the distributive property to expand the first expression. $3(2g - 4) = 3(2g) - 3(4)$ $= 6g - 12$	**STEP 1** Factor the first expression. The GCF of 25 and 20 is 5. $25 + 20t = 5(5) + 5(4t)$ $= 5(5 + 4t)$
STEP 2 Compare the expanded expression to the second expression. They are the same, so they are equivalent.	**STEP 2** Compare the factored expression to the second expression. They are not the same, so they are not equivalent.
So, you can write $3(2g - 4) = 6g - 12$.	So, you can write $25 + 20t \neq 5(6 + 4t)$.

✔ Quick Check
Choose an equivalent expression.

1 $8a - 4$ is equivalent to _____.

 a) $4(2a - 1)$ **b)** $2(8a - 4)$ **c)** $3(5a - 1)$ **d)** $4(2a + 1)$

2 $12 + 3y$ is equivalent to _____.

 a) $6(2 + 3y)$ **b)** $12(1 + y)$ **c)** $3(4 + y)$ **d)** $4(3 + 2y)$

Practice on Your Own
Choose an equivalent expression.

3 $4n - 10$ is equivalent to _____.

 a) $4(n - 5)$ **b)** $5(2n - 2)$ **c)** $2(n - 5)$ **d)** $2(2n - 5)$

4 $11(3d - 6)$ is equivalent to _____.

 a) $33d - 6$ **b)** $33d - 66$ **c)** $3d - 66$ **d)** $11d - 66$

5 $30 + 18p$ is equivalent to _____.

 a) $6(5 + 3p)$ **b)** $2(15 + 3p)$ **c)** $3(5p + 6)$ **d)** $3(10 + 3p)$

6 $8(7r + 2)$ is equivalent to _____.

 a) $56r + 16$ **b)** $15r + 10$ **c)** $56r + 2$ **d)** $7r + 16$

Write Algebraic Expressions for Unknown Quantities

TEACHING STRATEGY

1. **Vocabulary** Make sure students understand the terms *variable* and *expression*. If students confuse the terms *expression* and *equation*, ask a volunteer to explain the difference. Students should recognize that an equation contains an equal sign, while an expression does not.

2. **Teach** Explain that an algebraic expression is a mathematical way of writing a word phrase. Tell students that in order to connect words with algebra, it is important that they learn to associate key words with the correct operation. Offer examples of simple phrases and real-life situations. **Ask** What operation is described in the phrase *the product of x and 18*? Explain. [Multiplication; The key word *product* indicates multiplication is used and *x* and 18 are the factors in the expression.] **Ask** If you are *a* years old and your cousin is 4 years younger than you, what expression could you write to show your cousin's age? [$a - 4$] **Ask** If you own *b* number of books and your friend owns 7 more than you do, what expression could you write to show how many books your friend has? [$b + 7$]

3. **Quick Check** Look for this common error as students solve the Quick Check exercises.
   - Using the wrong operation in an expression as a result of misunderstanding key words and the operations associated with them.

4. **Next Steps** Assign the practice exercises to students who show understanding. For students who need more support, provide tutoring using the alternate teaching strategy.

Additional Teaching Resource
 Online Transition Guide with Reteach and Extra Practice worksheets from previous grade levels

ALTERNATE INTERVENTION STRATEGY

Materials: index cards

Strategy: Use index cards to write algebraic expressions for a word expression.

1. Write on each index card a numerical expression such as: $9 + 2$, $11 - 6$, $8 \cdot 7$, and $30 \div 5$.

2. Divide students into groups of four.
   - Have one student hold up an index card.
   - Have each student in the group read aloud the expression.
   - Try to get students to use as many different phrases as possible. For example, $9 + 2$ can be read as *9 plus 2, the sum of 9 and 2, 2 added to 9, 2 more than 9*, and so on.
   - Ask students to record each phrase on an index card.

3. For each expression, have students replace one of the numbers with a variable. For example:
   $a + 2$, $11 - b$, $8 \cdot t$, and $m \div 5$.

4. Again, have students in each group read the expression aloud using different phrases. Record each phrase on an index card.

5. Remove the algebraic expressions. Distribute the index cards with the algebraic expressions in word form and have students write the algebraic form.

Write Algebraic Expressions for Unknown Quantities

Example 1

Write an algebraic expression for the following.

The product of x and 87

The word *product* indicates multiplication. So, x and 87 are multiplied together: $x \cdot 87$.

A product of a variable and a number can be rewritten as a single term. Usually the number (coefficient) is written before the variable.

So, an expression is $87x$.

Example 2

Write an algebraic expression for the following.

Cora is 8 years older than Leon.

If Cora is 8 years older than Leon, her age is 8 years more than Leon's age. This indicates addition.

When Leon is 5 years old, Cora will be $(5 + 8) = 13$ years old. When Leon is y years old, Cora will be $y + 8$ years old.

So, an expression is $y + 8$.

✔ Quick Check

x is an unknown number. Write an expression for each of the following.

1 Quotient of the number and 22

_____

2 6 more than the number

_____

3 13 less than the number

_____

4 Product of the number and 19

_____

Practice on Your Own
x is an unknown number. Write an expression for each of the following.

5 Product of 72 and the number

_____

6 Quotient of the number and 12

_____

7 8 less than twice the number

_____

8 1.5 more than the number

_____

9 12 less than 3 times the number

_____

10 1 more than half the number

_____

Solve Algebraic Equations by Balancing

TEACHING STRATEGY

1. **Vocabulary** Review the term *inverse operation*. Explain that inverse means "opposite." Remind students that the inverse, or opposite, of addition is subtraction. **Ask** What is the inverse of division? [multiplication] Also review the concept of *balancing*. Ask students to visualize a balance scale and remind them that in order to keep the scale balanced, the same mass must be added or removed from *both* sides.

2. **Teach** Explain to students that they can apply the addition, subtraction, division, or multiplication property of equality to solve an equation. Remind them that according to the addition property of equality, if you add the same number to both sides of an equation, the two sides will remain equal. Direct students to Example 1. **Ask** What operation does the equation show? [subtraction] **Ask** Which operation is the inverse of subtraction? [addition] Guide students through the example, highlighting the fact that the same number is added to both sides of the equation. Have check their answer by substituting 11 for x in the original equation: $11 - 4 = 7$, which is true. Repeat the process for Example 2, noting how the division property of equality is used.

3. **Quick Check** Look for these common errors as students solve the Quick Check exercises.
   - Using the operation found in the equation, instead of the inverse operation.
   - Operating on only one side of the equation, indicating a lack of understanding of the concept of balancing.

Additional Teaching Resource
🖱 Online Transition Guide with Reteach and Extra Practice worksheets from previous grade levels

ALTERNATE INTERVENTION STRATEGY

Materials: algebra tiles or TRT6 (Algebra Tiles)

Strategy: Use models to solve algebraic equations.

1. Write the equation $x - 3 = 5$ on the board.

2. Have students use algebra tiles to model $x - 3 = 5$. **Ask** How many x tiles are on the left side? [1] How many -1 tiles are on the left side? [3] How many $+1$ tiles are on the right side? [5] After students have modeled the equation, draw the model on the board.

3. Ask What do you need to do to get the x tile alone on the left side? [Add three $+1$ tiles to the left side and three $+1$ tiles to the right side.]

4. Write $x - 3 + 3 = 5 + 3$ on the board. Guide students to use algebra tiles to model the revised equation, and then draw the model on the board.

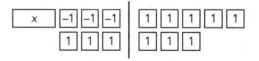

5. Ask How does adding three $+1$ tiles isolate the x on the left side? [The three $+1$s and the three -1s add up to zero, so they cancel each other out.] Have students remove these six tiles. **Ask** What algebraic term represents the x tile? [x] How many $+1$ tiles are on the right side now? [8] What simplified equation represents the tiles? [$x = 8$] Write the equation on the board.

6. Repeat this process with $2x = 10$ and $x + 4 = 8$. Once students are comfortable using algebra tiles to model equations, have them solve $x + 2 = 11$ without tiles.

EE
SKILL 23 # Solve Algebraic Equations by Balancing

You can use inverse operations to solve an equation. This is also called *balancing an equation*.

STEP 1 Get the variable alone on one side of the equation. To do that, you add, subtract, multiply, or divide both sides of the equation by the same nonzero number.

STEP 1 Simplify the equation.

Example 1 **Addition or subtraction**

Solve the equation.
$$x - 4 = 7$$

$x - 4 = 7$

$x - 4 + \mathbf{4} = 7 + \mathbf{4}$ Add 4 to both sides.

$x = 11$ Simplify the equation.

Example 2 **Multiplication or division**

Solve the equation.
$$\frac{1}{4}x = 12$$

$\frac{1}{4}x = 12$

$\frac{1}{4}x \div \frac{1}{4} = 12 \div \frac{1}{4}$ Divide both sides by $\frac{1}{4}$.

$\frac{1}{4}x \cdot \frac{4}{1} = 12 \cdot \frac{4}{1}$ Multiply both sides by the reciprocal of $\frac{1}{4}$.

$x = 48$ Simplify the equation.

✔ Quick Check
Solve each equation.

1 $x + 3 = 12$

2 $x - 7 = 1$

3 $5x = 75$

_____   _____   _____

Practice on Your Own
Solve each equation.

4 $\frac{2}{5}x = 20$

5 $x + \frac{1}{4} = 1$

6 $x + 7.5 = 12$

_____   _____   _____

7 $x - \frac{3}{4} = 4$

8 $x - 13 = 21$

9 $1.1x = 3.3$

_____   _____   _____

EE SKILL 24
Solve Algebraic Equations by Substitution

TEACHING STRATEGY

1. **Vocabulary** Review the meaning of substitute. Ask What are other ways to say, "Substitute 2 for x?" [Possible answers: Use 2 instead of x. Replace x with 2.] Remind students that an equation is a statement that the values of two mathematical expressions are equal. Review the symbols for equal (=) and not equal (≠).

2. **Teach** Explain to students that the substitution method involves replacing the variable in an equation with a number that could possibly be the solution. Point out that substitution is a trial-and-error method. It requires trying values in the equation until a solution is found. Direct students to the beginning of Example 1. **Ask** Which number is first substituted for x? [1] Why is 1 not the solution? [because 1 + 4 equals 5, not 7] Encourage students to apply logical thinking to the process of substitution. Guide them to deduce that since 7 is two greater than 5, then the value of x should also be two greater than the substituted number, 1. The number that is two greater than 1 is 3, which is the solution. Direct students to Example 2 and repeat the process.

3. **Quick Check** Look for this common error as students solve the Quick Check exercises.
   - Listing incorrect answers, indicating computation errors due to a lack of proficiency with basic addition, subtraction, multiplication, and division facts.

4. **Next Steps** Assign the practice exercises to students who show understanding. For students who need more support, provide tutoring using the alternate teaching strategy.

Additional Teaching Resource
Online Transition Guide with Reteach and Extra Practice worksheets from previous grade levels

ALTERNATE INTERVENTION STRATEGY

Materials: algebra tiles or TRT6 (Algebra Tiles)

Strategy: Use models to solve algebraic equations.

1. Write the equation $p + 2 = 14$ on the board.

2. Have students follow the steps below to model the equation using algebra tiles.

3. First have them model the right side of the equation using fourteen 1 tiles. **Ask** How many 1 tiles should you place on the left side to represent the number 2 in the equation $p + 2 = 14$? [2]

4. Remind students that because both sides of an equation must be equal, p represents the number of units needed to make the left side of the equation equal to 14.

5. Then have students think about how many more 1 tiles they will need to add to the left side to get 14 tiles in all. Guide them to deduce that since there are already 2 tiles on the left side, the missing number of the tiles must be fewer than 14 but more than 2. Ask students to place the tiles they add in a separate row below the 2 tiles that are already there. Have them count up to 14 (starting with 3) as they add tiles, one by one, to the row. When students have counted up to 14, have them say how many tiles they just added to the new row [12]. Tell students that because both sides are now equal, 12 represents the value of p in the equation $p + 2 = 14$. Since $12 + 2 = 14$, the solution of the equation is 12.

6. Repeat this process with $x + 5 = 13$. Once students are comfortable using the tiles to model equations, have them solve $y - 9 = 2$ without the use of algebra tiles.

Solve Algebraic Equations by Substitution

Example 1

Solve the equation. $x + 4 = 7$

If $x = $ **1**, $x + 4 = $ **1** $+ 4$ Substitute **1** for x.

$\qquad\qquad = 5$ $5 \neq 7$, so **1** is not a solution.

If $x = $ **3**, $x + 4 = $ **3** $+ 4$ Substitute **3** for x.

$\qquad\qquad = 7$ $7 = 7$, so **3** is a solution.

The equation $x + 4 = 7$ is true when $x = 3$.

So, 3 is the solution of the equation $x + 4 = 7$.

Example 2

Solve the equation. $2x - 1 = 9$

If $x = $ **4**, $2x - 1 = (2 \cdot $ **4**$) - 1$ Substitute **4** for x.

$\qquad\qquad\quad = 8 - 1$

$\qquad\qquad\quad = 7$ $7 \neq 9$, so **4** is not a solution.

If $x = $ **5**, $2x - 1 = (2 \cdot $ **5**$) - 1$ Substitute **5** for x.

$\qquad\qquad\quad = 10 - 1$

$\qquad\qquad\quad = 9$ $9 = 9$, so **5** is a solution.

The equation $2x - 1 = 9$ is true when $x = 5$.

So, 5 is the solution of the equation $2x - 1 = 9$.

✔ Quick Check
State whether each statement is True or False.

1 7 is the solution of the equation $x + 1 = 9$.   _____

2 3 is the solution of the equation $3n + 3 = 12$.   _____

3 18 is the solution of the equation $\frac{y}{3} = 5$.   _____

Practice on Your Own
State whether each statement is True or False.

4 9 is the solution of the equation $11a + 1 = 100$.   _____

5 12.5 is the solution of the equation $w - 4.5 = 17$.   _____

6 20 is the solution of the equation $\frac{x}{4} = 5$.   _____

7 6 is the solution of the equation $\frac{y}{3} = \frac{2}{3}$.   _____

EE
SKILL 25
Graph Inequalities on a Number Line

<table>
<tr><th>TEACHING STRATEGY</th><th>ALTERNATE INTERVENTION STRATEGY</th></tr>
</table>

TEACHING STRATEGY

1. **Vocabulary** Review with students how to read and interpret these four inequality symbols: < (is less than), > (is greater than), ≤ (is less than or equal to), ≥ (is greater than or equal to).

2. **Teach** Explain that graphing an inequality on a number line means showing the numbers that make the inequality a true statement. Have students look at Example 1. **Ask** If x is less than 4.5, can x equal 6? [No.] Point to 5 and 6 and tell students that these numbers result in a false statement. Draw an open circle over 4.5 and explain that you must use an open circle because the inequality is <, not ≤. Draw an arrow from the open circle to the left. Tell students that the number line shows that all numbers less than 4.5 make the inequality true. For example, 3 < 4.5 is true, so 3 is a solution. Then have students look at Example 2. **Ask** Why do you use a shaded circle to graph this inequality? [The inequality uses ≥, not >, so $\frac{2}{3}$ is a solution of the inequality.] Why does the arrow in the graph point to the right? [Numbers greater than $\frac{2}{3}$ are also solutions.]

3. **Quick Check** Look for these common errors as students solve the Quick Check exercises.
   - Confusing the meaning of the four inequality symbols, resulting in incorrect graphs.
   - Forgetting when to use an open circle and when to use a shaded circle when graphing inequalities on a number line.

4. **Next Steps** Assign the practice exercises to students who show understanding. For students who need more support, provide tutoring using the alternate teaching strategy.

Additional Teaching Resource
Online Transition Guide with Reteach and Extra Practice worksheets from previous grade levels

ALTERNATE INTERVENTION STRATEGY

Materials: TRT1 (Number Lines), TRT46 (Inequality Cards), scissors

Strategy: Match inequalities to their graphs.

1. Cut out multiple copies of the cards shown below. Give each student one set of shuffled cards. Leave the cards face down.

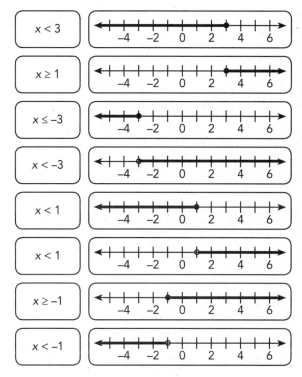

2. Tell students they are going to play "Speed." When you say "go," students should flip all their cards over and match the correct graph to the inequality. The student to correctly match all the cards wins. (Cards are matched in the order presented above.)

3. After students have played a few rounds of the game, write one or two inequalities on the board. Then have students graph the inequalities on blank number lines.

Graph Inequalities on a Number Line

Example 1

Graph the inequality $x < 4.5$ on a number line.

STEP 1 Locate 4.5 on the number line.

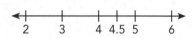

STEP 2 The inequality states that x is less than 4.5. Use an open circle at 4.5 to show that it is not a solution of the inequality.

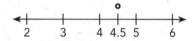

STEP 3 Draw an arrow to the left of 4.5 to indicate that all numbers less than 4.5 are solutions of the inequality.

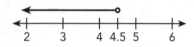

Example 2

Graph the inequality $t \geq \frac{2}{3}$ on a number line.

STEP 1 Locate $\frac{2}{3}$ on the number line.

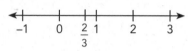

STEP 2 The inequality states that t is greater than or equal to $\frac{2}{3}$. Use a shaded circle at $\frac{2}{3}$ to show that it is a solution of the inequality.

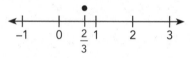

STEP 3 Draw an arrow to the right of $\frac{2}{3}$ to indicate that all numbers greater than or equal to $\frac{2}{3}$ are solutions of the inequality.

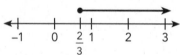

✔ Quick Check

Draw a number line to represent each inequality.

1 $p < 6$

2 $c \geq 5.5$

3 $f \leq -2$

4 $w > \frac{1}{2}$

5 $n > 11.5$

6 $j \leq 20$

Practice on Your Own
Draw a number line to represent each inequality.

7 $m \geq 18$

8 $g < \frac{3}{4}$

9 $r \leq 12.5$

10 $d > -7$

11 $x \geq 2\frac{1}{3}$

12 $b < 8.6$

Write Algebraic Inequalities

TEACHING STRATEGY

1. **Vocabulary** Remind students that in algebra an *inequality* states that two values are not equal. Explain that inequality relationships can be expressed algebraically using numbers and symbols, verbally using words, or graphically using a number line. Review the meanings of the symbols $\neq$, $>$, $<$, $\geq$, and $\leq$.

2. **Teach** Direct students to the table. Review the verbal descriptions for the algebraic inequality $p < 2$. **Ask** What is the verbal description for this inequality? [p is less than 2] Can the value of p be 3? Explain your answer. [The value of p must be less than 2; 3 is greater than 2, so p cannot be 3.] Repeat the process to review verbal descriptions for the other inequalities shown in the table.

3. **Quick Check** Look for these common errors as students solve the Quick Check exercises.
   - Consistently reversing inequality symbols due to confusion over the direction a symbol should open toward to show less than or greater than.
   - Use of $<$ instead of $\leq$ (or vice versa), or $>$ instead of $\geq$ (or vice versa), indicating a lack of understanding of when language indicates a given value is part of the solution set.

4. **Next Steps** Assign the practice exercises to students who show understanding. For students who need more support, provide tutoring using the alternate teaching strategy.

Additional Teaching Resource
Online Transition Guide with Reteach and Extra Practice worksheets from previous grade levels

ALTERNATE INTERVENTION STRATEGY

Materials: index cards, digital timer or clock with second hand

Strategy: Use index cards to practice pairing verbal descriptions with the corresponding algebraic inequalities.

1. Divide the class into pairs and distribute 24 index cards to each pair.

2. List the following six inequalities on the board: $x < 15$, $x > 15$, $x \leq 75$, $x \geq 75$, $x \geq 25$, $x \leq 25$. Have each student copy each inequality onto its own index card.

3. Begin with $x < 15$. Ask volunteers to suggest a verbal description of a real-world situation that could be represented by the inequality. [Possible answer: The restaurant host told us the wait for a table is less than 15 minutes.] Write each correct description on the board. Underline the key words in each description that directly relate to the inequality. (For the above sample, underline wait, *less than*, and *15 minutes*.)

4. Tell students to copy one of the correct descriptions onto an index card, not including the underlining.

5. Repeat the process for each of the other five inequalities.

6. Ask each student to shuffle the six cards on which they have written descriptions and exchange the cards with their partner.

7. At your signal, each student should match a set of inequality cards to the description cards received from his or her partner. Pairs compete to correctly match all six inequalities in the least amount of time.

8. Partners should check each other's work. The partner with the most correct matches wins. If both partners have the same number of correct matches, the partner with the faster time wins.

Name _____ Date _____

Write Algebraic Inequalities

Use the symbols >, <, and ≠ to compare quantities that are not equal.

Use the symbols ≥ and ≤ to compare quantities that may or may not be equal.

Verbal Description	Algebraic Inequality
The cost of a newspaper, n, **is not** $5.	$n \neq 5$
The cost of a pear, p, is less than $2	$p < 2$
The height of the window, h, is **at most** 6 feet. OR The height of the window, h, **is no more than** 6 feet. OR The height of the window, h, **is less than or equal** to 6 feet.	$h \leq 6$
The width of the book, w, is **more than** 3 inches.	$w > 3$
The weight of the desk, d, **is at least** 50 pounds. OR The weight of the desk, d, **is no less than** 50 pounds. OR The weight of the desk, d, **is greater than or equal** to 50 pounds.	$d \geq 50$

✔ Quick Check

Complete each ? with =, >, or <.

1 23 ? 32 _____

2 25 + 3 ? 22 + 2 _____

Use x to represent the unknown quantity.
Write an algebraic inequality for each statement.

3 The width of the hall is more than 4 feet. _____

4 No more than 10 people can ride the elevator at any given time. _____

Practice on Your Own
Complete each ? with =, >, or <.

5 −11 + 2 ? −16 + 7 _____

6 6 · (−3) ? −5 − 14 _____

Write an algebraic inequality for each statement.
Use x to represent the unknown quantity.

7 There are at least 25 students in the school orchestra. _____

8 The annual membership fee is less than $35. _____

9 The weight the shelf can support is at most 80 pounds. _____

10 The number of hours she worked last week was more than 24. _____

Compare Quantities Using a Ratio

TEACHING STRATEGY

1. **Vocabulary** On the worksheet, have students identify examples of the following terms: *ratio*, *term*, *greatest common factor (GCF)*, *simplest form*.

2. **Teach** For Example 1, begin by pointing out that there are three quantities identified in the problem. **Ask** Which quantity are we first asked to use? [the number of messages Alexis sent, 45] Which quantity are we asked to compare it to? [the number of messages Casey sent, 75] What is the greatest common factor of 45 and 75? [15] For Example 2, remind students that ratios can be written in three ways. **Ask** Which way is usually closest to the way the comparison is stated in the problem? [using the word "to"] Which way is easiest to write the ratio in simplest form? [as a fraction] What is the greatest common factor of 60 and 45? [15]

3. **Quick Check** Look for these common errors as students solve the Quick Check exercises.
   - Listing ratio terms in reverse order because they do not recognize that the order in which they are asked to compare quantities dictates the order of the terms.
   - Inability to recognize common factors of terms leading to failure to write ratio in simplest form.
   - Lack of proficiency with division facts leading to incorrect calculation of simplest form.

4. **Next Steps** Assign the practice exercises to students who show understanding. For students who need more support, provide tutoring using the alternate teaching strategy.

Additional Teaching Resource

 Online Transition Guide with Reteach and Extra Practice worksheets from previous grade levels

ALTERNATE INTERVENTION STRATEGY

Materials: TRT14 (Centimeter Grid Paper), colored pencils

Strategy: Use grid paper and colored pencils to correctly place the terms of a ratio, identify the GCF, and write the ratio in simplest form.

1. Write the following on the board.
   To build a cabinet, Sam used 16 screws and 48 nails. Write a ratio to compare the number of nails to the number of screws.

2. On plain paper, have students write "48 nails" in one color and "16 screws" in a second color. Ask students to use the first color to write the first quantity being compared (number of nails) in one cell on grid paper. Then, in the cell directly below that one, ask them to use the second color to write the second quantity being compared. Have them draw a fraction bar in black between the two numbers. Point out that $\frac{48}{16}$ is a ratio that compares the number of nails to the number of screws, but because 48 and 16 have common factors, it is not in simplest form.

3. On the grid paper, have students write out the prime factorization for each term.

48	=	2	·	2	·	2	·	2	·	3
16	=	2	·	2	·	2	·	2		

4. Have students read the paired factors from right to left to identify the GCF: $2 \cdot 2 \cdot 2 \cdot 2 = 16$. Divide both ratio terms by the GCF, 16, and using the same colors write the ratio in simplest form: $\frac{3}{1}$.

5. Work through other examples with students. (e.g. Use 56 nails and 21 screws.) As students become familiar with correctly placing ratio terms, switch from grid paper to plain paper.

Compare Quantities Using a Ratio

Example 1	**Write a Ratio**

One day Alexis sent 45 text messages, Casey sent 75, and Sara sent 60. Write a ratio to compare the number of text messages Alexis sent to the number Casey sent.

STEP 1 Write the ratio. A ratio has 2 terms.

Alexis   45 ← term

Casey   75 ← term

STEP 2 Express the ratio in simplest form.

$\frac{45}{75} = \frac{45 \div 15}{75 \div 15}$ Divide by the GCF.

$= \frac{3}{5}$

Example 2	**Write a Ratio Three Ways**

Use the data from Example 1. Write a ratio in three ways to compare the number of text messages Sara sent to the number Alexis sent.

STEP 1 Write the ratio 3 ways: using "to," using a colon, and as a fraction.

60 to 45   60 : 45 $\frac{45}{75}$

STEP 2 Express each ratio in simplest form by dividing each term by the GCF, 15.

4 to 3   4 : 3 $\frac{3}{5}$

☑ Quick Check

Write a ratio in simplest form three ways to compare quantities.

Juan recycled 42 plastic bottles, 28 cans, and 35 glass bottles.

1 number of glass bottles to number of plastic bottles _____

2 number of cans to number of plastic bottles _____

Practice on Your Own
Write a ratio in simplest form to compare quantities.

After the 2010 Census, eight states gained seats in the U.S. House of Representatives. The table below shows how many representatives each of these states will now have. Write ratios to compare the number of state representatives.

Arizona	9
Florida	28
Georgia	14
Nevada	4

South Carolina	7
Texas	36
Utah	4
Washington	10

3 Arizona to Texas _____

4 Washington to Nevada _____

5 Utah to Florida _____

6 Texas to Arizona _____

7 Georgia to South Carolina _____

8 Washington to Texas _____

© Marshall Cavendish International (Singapore) Private Limited.

RP
SKILL 28 # Recognize Equivalent Ratios

TEACHING STRATEGY

1. **Vocabulary** On the worksheet, have students identify examples of the following vocabulary terms: *equivalent ratios*, *common factors*, *simplest form*. Ask students to explain how common factors are used to rewrite a ratio in simplest form.

2. **Teach** For Example 1, explain that division can only be used to find an equivalent ratio when the original ratio is not in simplest form. **Ask** What other factors could you divide 6 and 36 by? [2 or 3] What would the equivalent ratios be? [3 : 18; 2 : 12] For Example 2, remind students that they can use any number (except 0 or 1) to multiply by as long as they use the same number for both terms. **Ask** What will happen if you multiply each term by 5? [You will get the equivalent ratio 30 : 180.]

3. **Quick Check** Look for these common errors as students solve the Quick Check exercises.
   - Inability to recognize common factors of terms, leading to failure to recognize whether a ratio is in simplest form.
   - Multiplying or dividing the terms of the ratio by different numbers, indicating a misunderstanding of equivalence.
   - Lack of proficiency with multiplication facts and division facts leading to incorrect calculation of equivalent ratios.

4. **Next Steps** Assign the practice exercises to students who show understanding. For students who need more support, provide tutoring using the alternate teaching strategy.

Additional Teaching Resource
Online Transition Guide with Reteach and Extra Practice worksheets from previous grade levels

ALTERNATE INTERVENTION STRATEGY

Materials: two-color counters

Strategy: Use the counters from the Manipulative Kit to model equivalent ratios using division or multiplication.

1. Distribute the counters. On the board, write 4 : 8. Have students use the counters to model the ratio, using one color for the first quantity and the other color for the second.

2. Help students determine whether the ratio is in simplest form. **Ask** Besides 1, do 4 and 8 have any common factors? [Yes, 2 and 4.] Remind students they can write an equivalent ratio by dividing both quantities by the same common factor.

3. Tell students to divide each quantity of counters into 4 equal groups, then discard all but one group of each quantity. **Ask** When you divide both terms in the ratio 4 : 8 by 4, what equivalent ratio is the result? [1 : 2] On the board, above 4 : 8, write "1 : 2." Point out that 4 : 8 and 1 : 2 are equivalent ratios. **Ask** Besides 1, do 1 and 2 have any common factors? [No.] And what does that tell you about the ratio 1 : 2? [It is in simplest form.]

4. Have students use the counters to model the ratio 4 : 8 again. Remind students they also can write an equivalent ratio by multiplying both quantities by the same number—any number except 0 or 1.

5. Tell students to multiply each quantity of counters by 2. Use more counters to model this. **Ask** When you multiply both terms in the ratio 4 : 8 by 2, what equivalent ratio is the result? [8 : 16] On the board, below 4 : 8, write "8 : 16." Point out that 1 : 2, 4 : 8, and 8 : 16 are all equivalent ratios.

6. Repeat the process by modeling other ratios and finding ratios equivalent to them.

Recognize Equivalent Ratios

Example 1   Using Division

Use division to find a ratio equivalent to 6 : 36.

STEP 1   Identify common factors of the terms.

Factors of 6: **1, 2, 3, 6**

Factors of 36: **1, 2, 3,** 4, **6,** 9, 12, 18, 36

Common factors: 1, 2, 3, 6

STEP 2   Divide each term in the ratio by one of the common factors. Do not use 1.

6 : 36 and 1 : 6 are equivalent ratios.

Example 2   Using Multiplication

Use multiplication to find a ratio equivalent to 6 : 36.

Multiply each term in the ratio by the same number. Do not use 0 or 1.

6 : 36 and 12 : 72 are equivalent ratios.

So, 1 : 6, 6 : 36, and 12 : 72 are all equivalent ratios. 1 : 6 is in simplest form because 1 and 6 have no common factors except 1.

✔Quick Check

Tell whether each pair of ratios are equivalent.

1 3 : 9 and 9 : 18 _____

2 $\frac{3}{9}$ and $\frac{9}{27}$ _____

Tell whether each ratio is in simplest form. Then write two ratios that are equivalent to the given ratio.

3 6 : 8 _____

4 3 to 7 _____

5 6 to 10 _____

Practice on Your Own

Tell whether each ratio is in simplest form. Then write two ratios that are equivalent to the given ratio.

6 $\frac{2}{5}$ _____

7 $\frac{6}{27}$ _____

8 $\frac{1}{8}$ _____

9 4 : 6 _____

10 21 : 8 _____

11 4 : 15 _____

12 24 to 72 _____

13 30 to 6 _____

14 6 to 16 _____

Find Rates and Unit Rates

TEACHING STRATEGY

1. **Vocabulary** Make sure students understand the terms *rate* and *unit rate*. Remind them that a rate compares two quantities that have different units. Also point out that a unit rate compares a quantity to one unit of another quantity.

2. **Teach** Direct students to Example 1. Point out that average speed is a particular type of unit rate. **Ask** What two quantities are being compared in this example? [distance in miles and time in hours] Direct students to Step 1. **Ask** What is the rate at which Nia drove? [225 miles in 5 hours] Direct students to Step 2. **Ask** How do we find the average speed, the unit rate, at which Nia drove? [Divide 225 by 5.] Direct students to Example 2. Explain that a unit price is a particular type of unit rate. Tell them that calculating unit prices is a very useful skill when shopping. Have students suggest other types of products where finding the unit rate might be helpful.

3. **Quick Check** Look for these common errors as students solve the Quick Check exercises.
   - Reversing the terms in a rate, indicating students need to review the wording of the problem.
   - Dividing both terms by a common factor that does not yield a denominator of 1, indicating a lack of understanding of the concept of unit rate.

4. **Next Steps** Assign the practice exercises to students who show understanding. For students who need more support, provide tutoring using the alternate teaching strategy.

Additional Teaching Resource

 Online Transition Guide with Reteach and Extra Practice worksheets from previous grade levels

ALTERNATE INTERVENTION STRATEGY

Materials: two-color counters

Strategy: Use counters to model how to find unit rates.

1. Distribute the counters. Tell students that two stalls at a farmers' market sell green beans. They need to determine which stall offers the better price. On the board, write:

   Spring Hill: $10 for 2 pounds
   Clover Farms: $12 for 3 pounds

2. Have students use counters to model Spring Hill's rate, using 10 counters of one color to model $10, and below it, use 2 counters of the other color to model 2 pounds. **Ask** What number must be on the bottom of a rate for it to be a unit rate? [1] What number do we need to divide by to make the bottom quantity equal to 1? [2] And if we divide the bottom quantity of the rate by 2, what must we do to the top quantity in the rate? {Divide it by 2 also.]

3. Have students divide each set of counters into two groups, then discard one group of each color. **Ask** What is the unit price, the price per pound, for beans at the Spring Hill stall? [$5 per lb]

4. Have students repeat the process to model the rate for Clover Farms' beans, then find the unit price. **Ask** What is the unit price, the price per pound, for beans at the Clover Farms stall? [$4 per lb] At which stall are the beans less expensive? [Clover Farms]

5. Repeat the process for other problem situations by using counters to first model the rates and then the corresponding unit rates.

Find Rates and Unit Rates

Example 1 **Finding Unit Rates**

Nia drove 225 miles in 5 hours. Find her average speed in miles per hour.

STEP 1 Write the rate. Label the terms.

$$\frac{225}{5} \begin{array}{l} \leftarrow \text{ miles} \\ \leftarrow \text{ hours} \end{array}$$

STEP 2 Use the unitary method to find the unit rate, the average number of miles Nia drove in 1 hour.

5 hours ← 225 miles

1 hour ← $\frac{225}{5}$ = 45 miles per hour

Nia drove at an average speed of 45 mi/h.

Example 2 **Comparing Unit Rates**

The price of cereal at two stores is shown. At which store is the cereal less expensive?

Store A: $3.29 for a 12-oz box
Store B: $5.00 for an 18-oz box

STEP 1 Find the unit price at each store.

Store A: $\frac{\$5.00}{12} \approx \$0.27$ per oz

Store B: $\frac{\$5.00}{18} \approx \$0.28$ per oz

STEP 2 Compare the unit prices.
$0.27 < $0.28

The cereal is less expensive at Store A.

✔ Quick Check
Solve.

1 A cyclist rode 36 miles in 4 hours. What was her average speed in miles per hour?

_____

2 Mr. Leonard paid $35.75 for 10 gallons of gas. At another gas station, Ms. Lu paid $36.90 for 11 gallons. Who got the better deal?

_____

Practice on Your Own
Solve.

3 A 5-pound bag of white onions costs $4.25. A 5-pound bag of red onions costs $4.45. Find the unit prices for each.

_____

4 The Write-On Company sells packs of 3 pens for $1.50. The Ink Company sells packs of 7 pens for $3.50. Find the unit price for each.

_____

5 Jenna drove 298 miles in 5 hours. Barry drove 238 miles in 4 hours. Who was driving at a greater average speed?

_____

6 Julieta bought $\frac{1}{4}$ lb of bologna for $1.50, 1 lb of ham for $7.00, and $\frac{1}{2}$ lb of salami for $3.99. Which deli meat cost the most per pound?

_____

Identify and Plot Coordinates

TEACHING STRATEGY

1. **Vocabulary** Using the worksheet, have students identify examples of the following terms: *coordinates, x-coordinate, y-coordinate, x-axis, y-axis, ordered pair,* and *origin.*

2. **Teach** Work through the example with students. **Ask** Why is the point *O* at (0, 0) called the origin? [It is where you start, or *originate*, to locate points in the coordinate plane.] **Ask** Which coordinate in an ordered pair shows the distance along the *x*-axis from the origin? [the first] **Ask** Which coordinate in an ordered pair shows the distance along the *y*-axis from the origin? [the second] Then, direct students to Step 3. To locate *B*, move right 7 units along the *x*-axis and up 1 unit in the direction of the *y*-axis. **Ask** What information displayed on the coordinate plane shows direction? [The arrows on the axes show direction.] In which direction does the x-axis point? [to the right] In which direction does the y-axis point? [up]

3. **Next Steps** Look for these common errors as students solve the Quick Check exercises.
   • Switching the *x*- and *y*-coordinates, indicating a misunderstanding of coordinate notation.
   • Not understanding the location of the 0 coordinates at the origin as they relate to the *x*- or *y*-axis, indicating confusion about the role of the axes.

4. Next Steps Assign the practice exercises to students who show understanding. For students who need more support, provide tutoring using the alternate teaching strategy.

Additional Teaching Resource
Online Transition Guide with Reteach and Extra Practice worksheets from previous grade levels

ALTERNATE INTERVENTION STRATEGY

Materials: TRT2 (Number Cards), red and blue pencils, TRT11 (Coordinate Grid) for display and TRT12 (Coordinate Grids)

Strategy: Create ordered pairs to identify and plot points in the coordinate plane.

1. Have each group of students create two decks of number cards from 1 to 10. Have them shade one set in red and the other in blue.

2. Display a coordinate plane that is easily accessible to students.

3. Explain to students that the "red" numbers are the *x*-coordinates and the "blue" numbers are the *y*-coordinates.

4. Have students draw a card from each deck to create an ordered pair. Ask them to explain which coordinate comes first and which comes second. [red *x*-coordinate comes first, blue *y*-coordinate comes second]

5. After students have correctly identified the ordered pair, have them plot the coordinates as a point on the coordinate plane. They can label the point with the initial of their last name.

6. Ask students to explain the process for plotting a point. Guide them with questions, such as "What does the first coordinate tell you to do?" [Move right from the origin along the *x*-axis.] "What does the second coordinate tell you to do? [Move up in the direction of the *y*-axis.]

7. Continue to have students draw cards to form ordered pairs until all cards have been used.

Identify and Plot Coordinates

Example

Use the coordinate plane at the right to identify and plot points.

STEP 1 Note the coordinates of point O, the origin: (0, 0).

STEP 2 To Identify the location of the given point A, start at the origin. Count 4 units to the right, along the x-axis. Then count 6 units up to end at A. So the x-coordinate of point A is 4, and the y-coordinate is 6. Written together as an ordered pair, the coordinates of point A are (4, 6).

STEP 3 Plot point B at (7, 1) on the coordinate plane: Start at the origin, then count 7 units right and 1 unit up. Mark and label point B.

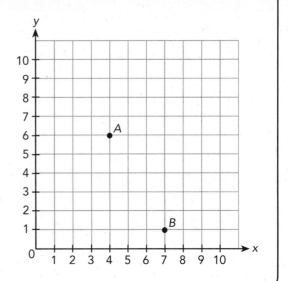

✓ Quick Check

Use the coordinate plane at the right. Give the coordinates of each point.

1 C_____

2 D_____

3 E_____

4 F_____

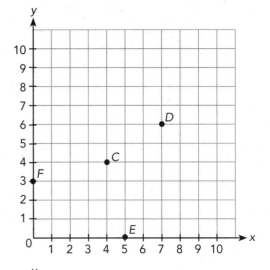

Practice on Your Own

Use the coordinate plane at the right. Give the coordinates of each point.

5 G_____

6 H_____

Plot the following points on the coordinate plane.

8 J(0, 1)

8 K(5, 6)

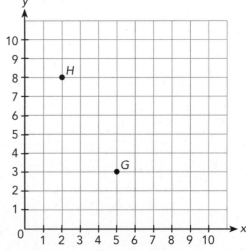

Solve Percent Problems

TEACHING STRATEGY

1. **Vocabulary** Make sure students understand the meaning of the term *percent* and recognize the percent symbol. Explain that percent comes from the Latin phrase *per centum*, which means "out of 100." *Per centum* entered the English language in the 16th century. It was commonly abbreviated as "per cent." Point out that the percent symbol includes two open circles, a reminder of the two zeros in the number 100. Also remind students that the *unitary method* of solving problems involves identifying the value of 1 unit of a quantity, then multiplying that value of a single unit to determine the value of any number of multiple units.

2. **Teach** Read the problem in Example 1. **Ask** What are we asked to find? [how much 70% of 2,400 is] Explain that bar models can be very useful when solving percent problems. Direct students to the bar model. Point out that each labeled part of the bar has two values associated with it, an amount and a percent. Tell students that, when drawing a bar model to represent a percent problem, they should begin by labeling the whole bar "100%," as this bar is labeled at top. **Ask** Do we know what amount is equal to 100% in this problem? [Yes, 100% of the seats in the theater is 2,400 seats.] Point out that the whole bar is labeled with two values: 2,400 seats and 100%. **Ask** How many parts is the bar divided into? [2] What percent of the whole does the shaded part of the bar represent? [the 70% of the theater's seats that are filled for this

performance of the play] Point out that it is this amount that we are asked to find. **Ask** What percent of the whole does the unshaded part of the bar represent? [the 30% of the theater's seats that are not filled for this performance of the play] How do we know that 30% of the seats are not filled? [70% of the theater's seats are filled, and 100% − 70% = 30%.] Point out that we do not know the number of seats that are empty, and we do not need to know that to determine how many seats are filled.

Direct students to the use of the unitary method in Example 1. **Ask** For which of the three percent values shown in the bar model do we know the number of seats? [100% is equal to 2,400 seats.] Point out that because we know that 100% is equivalent to 2,400 seats, it is the first step we write when we use the unitary method. **Ask** If 100% is equal to 2,400 seats, how can we find the value of 1 unit, of 1%? [Divide 2,400 by 100.] How many seats is 1% of the seats in the theater? [24] So, how many seats is 70% of the seats in the whole theater? [70 × 24 = 1,680 seats.]

Direct students to Example 2. **Ask** What does the whole bar represent in this model? [the original price of the shirt] Do we know what dollar amount is equal to 100%? {No.] For what percent of the bar do we know a dollar amount? [85% of the bar is the sale price of the shirt, $17.]

3. **Quick Check** Look for these common errors as students solve the Quick Check exercises.
   - Assigning the wrong number value from the problem to 100%, indicating confusion about the concept of percent.
   - In the unitary method, confusing the divisor and dividend, resulting in miscalculation of the value of a single unit.

Additional Teaching Resource

 Online Transition Guide with Reteach and Extra Practice worksheets from previous grade levels

Name _____ Date _____

Solve Percent Problems

Example 1 Finding a Part

A theater has 2,400 seats. For a performance of a play, it is 70% full. How many seats are filled?

First, draw a bar model that relates the number of seats to percent values.

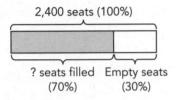

2,400 seats (100%)

? seats filled   Empty seats
(70%)   (30%)

From the bar model, use the unitary method.

$100\% \rightarrow 2,400$

$1\% \rightarrow \dfrac{2,400}{100} = 24$

$70\% \rightarrow 70 \times 24 = 1,680$

1,680 of the seats in the theater are filled.

Example 2 Finding the Whole

Bala paid $17 for a shirt. It was on sale for 15% off. What was the original price of the shirt?

The shirt was 15% off. Since 100% − 15% = 85%, the sale price was 85% of the original price.

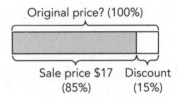

Original price? (100%)

Sale price $17   Discount
(85%)   (15%)

From the bar model, use the unitary method.

$85\% \rightarrow \$17$

$1\% \rightarrow \dfrac{17}{85} = \$0.20$

$100\% \rightarrow 100 \times \$0.20 = \$20$

The original price of the shirt was $20.

✓ Quick Check
Find the quantity represented by each percent.

1 80% of $360 _____

2 125% of 48 _____

3 36% of $690 _____

4 215% of 68 _____

Practice on Your Own
Find the quantity represented by each percent.

5 4% of 196 _____

6 72% of 900 _____

7 135% of $520 _____

8 37.5% of 8,888 _____

Solve.

9 At a park, 20% of employees are rangers. There are 7 rangers. How many people are employed at the park?

_____

10 A hotel room is priced at $125 per night. A 6% sales tax is added to the price. How much does one night at the hotel cost, including tax?

_____

Classify Angles

TEACHING STRATEGY

1. **Vocabulary** Make sure students understand the terms *angle*, *ray*, and *vertex*. Direct students to the angle in the example. Point out that it is the space between the rays, and not the length of the rays, that determines the size of the angle. Tell students that when naming an angle using the vertex and points on the rays, the vertex is always the middle letter.

2. **Teach** Direct students to Step 1 of the example. **Ask** Why is it helpful to draw a vertical, dotted line up from vertex B? [Drawing a vertical line will form a right angle from which you can classify angles as acute or obtuse.] Direct students to Step 2 of the example. **Ask** What do you know about acute and obtuse angles? [Acute angles measure less than 90° and obtuse angles are greater than 90° but not more than 180°.] Draw a straight line. **Ask** What is the measure of this angle? [180°]

3. **Quick Check** Look for this common error as students solve the quick check exercises.
   • Confusing obtuse and acute angles due to confusion over the meanings of those two terms.

4. **Next Steps** Assign the practice exercises to students who show understanding. For students who need more support, provide tutoring using the alternate teaching strategy.

Additional Teaching Resource
🖱 Online Transition Guide with Reteach and Extra Practice worksheets from previous grade levels

ALTERNATE INTERVENTION STRATEGY

Materials: TRT47 (Angle Images), index cards

Strategy: Use a square corner to classify angles.

1. Distribute papers with the angle images and index cards to students. Explain that once they can identify the right angle, students can use the right angle as a guide to name or classify other angles.

2. Suggest students use the index card as a tester. Have students use their right-angle testers to identify angles larger or smaller than a right angle.

3. For a right angle, demonstrate how the edges of the tester align with the two rays.

4. Because an acute angle is smaller than a right angle, one of the rays will be hidden by the tester.

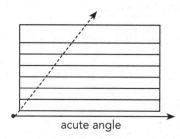

acute angle

5. For an obtuse angle, the space between the rays will be greater than the square corner on the tester.

6. A straight angle will align only along the bottom of the tester.

7. Change the position of the angles and test them again.

8. As students become more comfortable classifying angles, ask them to draw an example of each kind of angle.

Name _____ Date _____

Classify Angles

Example

An angle is formed by two rays that share a common endpoint called the vertex. In the angle at right, $\overrightarrow{BA}$ and $\overrightarrow{BC}$ meet at vertex B to form ∠ABC.

Angles are measured in degrees. The symbol used to show degrees is °. The measure of angle ABC is 25°. This is the same as writing m∠ABC = 25°.

Classify ∠ABC as an acute, obtuse, or right angle. Use the chart at right for reference.

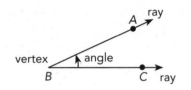

STEP 1 From vertex B, draw a dotted line perpendicular to $\overrightarrow{BC}$ to form a right angle.

STEP 2 Compare the measure of ∠ABC to the measure of the right angle you drew.

$$25° < 90°$$

So, ∠ABC is an acute angle.

Angle Type	Description
Acute	Measure is less than 90°.
Right	Measure is 90°.
Obtuse	Measure is greater than 90° but less than 180°.
Straight	Measure is 180°.

✔ Quick Check

Tell whether each angle is an acute, obtuse or right angle.

1 35°

2

3 m∠Z = 75° _____

4 m∠5 = 121° _____

Practice on Your Own

Tell whether each angle is an acute, obtuse or right angle.

5 135°

6 17°

7 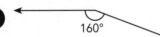 160°

8 92°

9 m∠R = 179° _____

10 m∠G = 89° _____

SKILL 33 Identify Parallel and Perpendicular Lines

TEACHING STRATEGY

1. **Vocabulary** Make sure students understand how to read and write the names of lines. Point out to students that a line containing the points X and Y can be written as $\overleftrightarrow{XY}$ or $\overleftrightarrow{YX}$.

2. **Teach** Direct students to Example 1. **Ask** What are the names of the lines? [line *CD* or *DC*, and line *MN* or *NM*] If the lines were extended forever in both directions, would they ever intersect? [No]. Would the distance between the lines ever change? [No.] Direct students to Example 2. **Ask** How do you know lines *AC* and *DB* form right angles? [There is a right-angle symbol at the point where the lines intersect.] Students should understand that perpendicular lines are a particular type of intersecting lines.

3. **Quick Check** Look for these common errors as students solve the Quick Check exercises.
   - Identifying all pairs of opposite sides of a figure as parallel, indicating a lack of understanding that line segments are sections of infinite lines and an inability to visualize the extension of those segments to see whether they will intersect.
   - Failing to distinguish perpendicular lines from other intersecting lines due to a lack of recognition that perpendicular lines intersect at right angles.

4. **Next Steps** Assign the practice exercise to students who show understanding. For students who need more support, provide tutoring using the alternate teaching strategy.

Additional Teaching Resource
Online Transition Guide with Reteach and Extra Practice worksheets from previous grade levels

ALTERNATE INTERVENTION STRATEGY

Materials: none

Strategy: Model parallel and perpendicular lines.

1. Have students point out pairs of lines in the classroom that are parallel. For example, they might mention the top edge of a wall and the bottom edge of the wall, the right and left edges of the board, or the horizontal lines on a sheet of lined writing paper.

2. **Ask** Can you hold your arms so that hey are parallel to each other? [Yes.] Have volunteers demonstrate how they can hold their arms parallel to each other. Given various student examples, point out that pairs of parallel lines can extend in any direction and that they always lie in the same plane.

3. Have students try to identify two lines in the room that intersect and form right angles. You may have to explain that right angles are angles that measure 90°. Encourage them to verify their assumptions by comparing the chosen angle to the corner of an index card.

4. Explain that lines that intersect to form 90° angles are perpendicular. Have students point out pairs of lines in the classroom that are perpendicular. For example, they might mention the corner of a book or desk, or a side and shelf of a set of bookshelves.

5. **Ask** Can you hold your arms so that hey are perpendicular to each other? [Yes.] Have volunteers demonstrate how they can hold their arms perpendicular to each other.

6. Have students identify other classroom examples of parallel lines and perpendicular lines.

Identify Parallel and Perpendicular Lines

Name _____ Date _____

Two lines in the same plane that do not intersect are parallel lines. Parallel lines are always
the same distance apart. They have no points in common.
Two lines that intersect and form a 90° angle are perpendicular lines.

Example 1 Parallel Lines

Lines $\overleftrightarrow{CD}$ and $\overleftrightarrow{MN}$ are parallel. They do not
intersect. They are the same distance apart. They
share no common points. The > symbols on the
lines indicate that $\overleftrightarrow{CD}$ and $\overleftrightarrow{MN}$ are parallel.

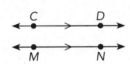

Example 2 Perpendicular Lines

Lines $\overleftrightarrow{AC}$ and $\overleftrightarrow{DB}$ are perpendicular. They
intersect to form 90° angles, as indicated by the
right angle symbol.

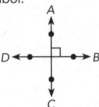

✔ Quick Check
Identify each pair of parallel line segments.

1
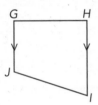

_____

2
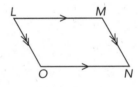

_____

Identify each pair of perpendicular line segments.

3 QRST is a square.

_____

4
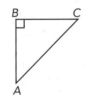

_____

Practice on Your Own
Identify each pair of parallel or perpendicular line segments.

5
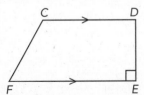

Parallel: _____

Perpendicular: _____

Classify Triangles by Side Lengths

TEACHING STRATEGY

1. **Vocabulary** You may want to explain the etymology of the terms equilateral, isosceles, and scalene. *Equilateral* comes from the Latin word *aequilaterus*, meaning "equal-sided." Isosceles comes from the Greek word *isoskeles*, meaning "equal leg." *Scalene* comes from the Greek word *skalenos*, meaning "unequal."

2. **Teach** Explain that triangles can be classified by their side lengths. Direct students to the three examples. First, focus on the side lengths of the triangles. **Ask** What type of triangle has three sides that are all equal in length? [equilateral triangle] What type of triangle has two sides that are equal in length? [isosceles triangle] What type of triangle has sides that are all unequal in length? [scalene triangle] Then, focus on the number of angles that have equal measures. **Ask** How many angles have equal measures in an equilateral triangle? [all three] If a triangle's angles measure 45°, 45°, and 90°, what type of triangle is it? [isosceles] How many angles have equal measures in a scalene triangle? [none]

3. **Quick Check** Look for these common errors as students solve the Quick Check exercises.
   - Classifying triangles based on the measures of the triangle's interior angles, not the number of angles that have equal measures.
   - Confusing the terms *equilateral*, isosceles, and *scalene*.

4. **Next Steps** Assign the practice exercises to students who show understanding. For students who need more support, provide tutoring using the alternate teaching strategy.

Additional Teaching Resource
🖱 Online Transition Guide with Reteach and Extra Practice worksheets from previous grade levels

ALTERNATE INTERVENTION STRATEGY

Materials: TRT 48 (Triangles), rulers

Strategy: Measure the sides lengths of triangles to classify them as equilateral, isosceles, or scalene

1. Copy the triangles and distribute them to students, along with rulers.

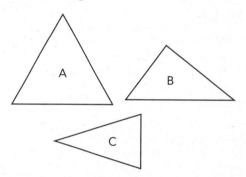

2. Have students measure and then record the side lengths of each triangle. Then, tell students to create a table like the one shown below. Have students look back at the measures of the side lengths they recorded for each triangle and count the number of sides that have equal measures. Instruct them to record this information in the second column of the table.

Triangle	Number of Equal Sides	Type of Triangle
A	[3]	[equilateral]
B	[0]	[scalene]
C	[2]	[isosceles]

3. Explain that an equilateral triangle has three sides of equal length, an isosceles triangle has at least two sides of equal length, and a scalene triangle has no sides that are equal in length. Have students complete the third column of the table using this information.

Name _____ Date _____

Classify Triangles by Side Lengths

Example 1 **Equilateral Triangle**

- All three sides have equal length.
- All three angles have equal measure.

Example 2 **Isosceles Triangle**

- At least two sides have equal length.
- The angles opposite the equal sides have equal measure.

Example 3 **Scalene Triangle**

- No sides have equal length.
- No angles have equal measure.

✔ Quick Check

Classify each triangle by its side lengths.

1

_____

2

_____

3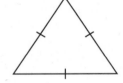

_____

Practice on Your Own
Classify each triangle by its side lengths.

4

_____

5

_____

6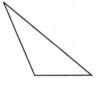

_____

Classify the triangle described below.

7 One angle measures 40° and a second angle measures 60°.

_____

Classify Triangles by Angle Measures

TEACHING STRATEGY

1. **Vocabulary** Review the terms *right*, *obtuse*, and *acute* in relation to angles. Remind students that a right angle measures 90°, an obtuse angle measures greater than 90°, and an acute angle measures less than 90°.

2. **Teach** Explain to students that triangles can be classified by the measures of their angles. Direct students to the examples. Remind students that the interior angles of a triangle have a sum of 180°. **Ask** Why can a right triangle only have one angle that measures 90°? [There are three interior angles in a triangle and the angles sum is 180°. If you had a triangle with two right angles, the third angle would have to measure 0°, which isn't possible.] How many obtuse angles must a triangle have to be classified as an obtuse triangle? [1] How many acute angles must a triangle have to be classified as an acute triangle? [3] Tell students that a triangle has two acute angles. **Ask** Can you classify the triangle based on this information? Explain. [No; the third angle could be acute, obtuse, or right, so it is impossible to classify the triangle.]

3. **Quick Check** Look for these common errors as students solve the Quick Check exercises.
   - Identifying an obtuse triangle or a right triangle as an acute triangle because it has two acute angles.
   - Confusing the terms acute and obtuse.

4. **Next Steps** Assign the practice exercises. For students who need more support, provide tutoring using the alternate teaching strategy.

Additional Teaching Resource
Online Transition Guide with Reteach and Extra Practice worksheets from previous grade levels

ALTERNATE INTERVENTION STRATEGY

Materials: index cards

Strategy: Name and classify angles in triangles as acute, obtuse, or right.

1. Draw an acute triangle, an obtuse triangle, and a right triangle on the board. Have students copy each triangle on a single sheet of paper.

2. Give each student an index card. Explain that the corners of the index card are right angles because they each measure 90°.

3. Beginning with the right triangle, have students use the index card to determine whether each angle in the right triangle is acute, obtuse, or right. If the angle is less than the angle formed by the corner of the index card, then the angle is acute. If the angle is greater than the angle formed by the card's corner, then the angle is obtuse. If the angle matches the angle of the corner, then the angle is right.

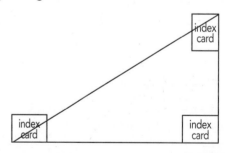

4. **Ask** How can you describe the three angles in this triangle? [There are two acute angles and one right angle.] Explain that this triangle is called a right triangle because one of the angles is a right angle.

5. Repeat the activity for the acute and obtuse triangles.

Name _____ Date _____

Classify Triangles by Angle Measures

Example 1 | **Right Triangle**

An angle that measures 90° is called a right angle.
Any triangle that includes a right angle is called a right triangle.

Example 2 | **Obtuse Triangle**

An angle with a measure greater than 90° is called an obtuse angle.
Any triangle that includes an obtuse angle is called an obtuse triangle.

Example 3 | **Acute Triangle**

An angle that measures less than 90° is called an acute angle.
Any triangle that includes three acute angles is called an acute triangle.

✓ Quick Check

Classify each triangle by its angle measures.

1

_____

2

_____

3

_____

Practice on Your Own
Classify each triangle by its angle measures.

4

_____

5
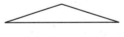

_____

6

_____

Classify the triangle described below.

7 None of the angles measure greater than 80°.

_____

Name Quadrilaterals

TEACHING STRATEGY

1. **Vocabulary** Make sure students understand the term *parallel*. Explain that parallel lines are lines that lie in the same plane, never intersect, and are always the same distance apart. Review the symbols used to show parallel sides and congruent sides and angles.

2. **Teach** Review the examples with students. Explain that these can be broken down into two major groups: parallelograms and trapezoids. Rectangles, rhombuses, and squares are special types of parallelograms. Furthermore, a square is a special type of rectangle, as well as a special type of rhombus. **Ask** Why are rectangles, rhombuses, and squares all examples of parallelograms? [A parallelogram has opposite sides that are parallel and equal in length, and opposite angles that are congruent. Rectangles, rhombuses, and squares all share these properties.] How is a trapezoid similar to a parallelogram? How is it different? [A trapezoid and parallelogram both have four sides. But a parallelogram has opposite sides that are equal in length and parallel, while a trapezoid has only one pair of parallel sides.]

3. **Quick Check** Look for these common errors as students solve the Quick Check exercises.

- Identifying adjacent sides of quadrilaterals as parallel, indicating confusion between marks showing parallelism and congruency.

- Confusing rhombuses and trapezoids, showing a lack of understanding of the properties of each quadrilateral.

Additional Teaching Resource

🖱 Online Transition Guide with Reteach and Extra Practice worksheets from previous grade levels

ALTERNATE INTERVENTION STRATEGY

Materials: TRT 49 (Figure and Property Cards), scissors

Strategy: Play a matching game to practice identifying properties of quadrilaterals.

1. Have students work in pairs. Tell each student-pair to create one set of figure- and property-cards.

One pair of parallel sides	Two pairs of parallel sides	All sides are the same length
Opposite sides are the same length	Opposite angles are equal in measure	All interior angles are right angles

2. One student in each pair should select a figure card. The other student should match the property card(s) with the figure, writing the statements on the back of the figure card as well as the name of the figure. Partners should take turns until all 5 figures have been identified.

3. You may wish to time the game to provide an extra challenge for students. The first pair to correctly identify the properties and names of all 5 figures wins the game.

G
SKILL 36
Name Quadrilaterals

Example 1 **Parallelogram**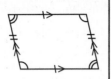
- Opposite sides are parallel and equal in length.
- Opposite angles have equal measures.

Example 2 **Rectangle**
- A rectangle is a type of parallelogram.
- All interior angles are right angles.
- Diagonals have equal measure.

Example 3 **Rhombus**
- A rhombus is a type of parallelogram.
- All sides are equal in length.
- Opposite angles have equal measure.
- Diagonals intersect at right angles.

Example 4 **Square**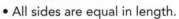
- A square is a type of parallelogram.
- All sides are equal in length.
- All interior angles are right angles.
- Diagonals have equal lengths.

Example 5 **Trapezoid**
- A trapezoid is not a parallelogram.
- Only one pair of opposite sides is parallel.

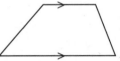

 Quick Check
Name each quadrilateral.

1

2

3

_____   _____   _____

Practice on Your Own
Name each quadrilateral.

4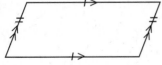

5

6

_____   _____   _____

Use a Protractor to Measure an Angle in Degrees

TEACHING STRATEGY

1. **Vocabulary** Make sure students understand the terms *ray*, *vertex*, and *angle*. Remind students that the measure of an angle is determined by the opening between the two rays that form its sides, not by the length of those rays.

2. **Teach** Direct students to the example. **Ask** What does a protractor measure? [angles] In what units is an angle measured? [degrees] What is the greatest angle measure that can be recorded by the protractor in the example? [180°] Direct students to Step 3 of the Example. **Ask** In which direction are the rays of angle *DEF* facing? [right] What scale will you read, the inner or outer scale? [inner] To help students remember which scale to use, tell them to think of where they would like to be on a cold, winter's day: RIGHT INside, not LEFT OUTside. Have students measure angle *DEF* again, this time aligning ray *ED* with the bottom of their protractors. **Ask** What is the measure of angle *DEF*? [25°] Explain to students that they can align the bottom of their protractor with either ray. The measurement will be the same.

3. **Quick Check** Look for this common error as students solve the Quick Check exercises.
   - Reading the inner scale of the protractor instead of the outer scale, or vice versa, yielding a reading that is the supplement of the correct measurement.

4. Assign the practice exercises to students who show understanding. For students who need more support, provide tutoring using the alternate teaching strategy.

Additional Teaching Resource
 Online Transition Guide with Reteach and Extra Practice worksheets from previous grade levels

ALTERNATE INTERVENTION STRATEGY

Materials: TRT20 (Clock), fastener, paper plate, scissors (Optional: demonstration clock)

Strategy: Use the hands on a clock to estimate the measure of an angle.

1. Cut out and assemble the clock on the paper plate with the hour hand at 12 and the minute hand at 3. **Ask** What kind of angle is formed when the hands of the clock are in this position? Explain. [Right angle; the hands are perpendicular to each other.] What is the measure of a right angle? [90°]

2. Have students look at the numbers between 12 and 3 on the clock. **Ask** How many equal sections are shown between 12 and 3? [3 equal sections] What is the measure of each section in degrees? [Possible answer: Each section is 30°. When the clock's hands are at 12 and 3, a 90° is formed. 90° ÷ 3 = 30°]

3. Ask What is the measure of the angle formed when the hour hand is at 1 and the minute hand is at 3? [60°] What is the measure of the angle formed when the hour hand is at 11 and the minute hand is at 3? [120°]

4. Work through additional examples with students that use the intervals between the whole numbers. For example, there are 6 intervals between 12 and 1 on the clock. Each interval measures 5°. **Ask** If the hour hand is on the 4th interval after 1 and the minute hand is at 4, what is the measure of the angle formed? [65°]

5. Pair students to work through five examples together. One student estimates the measure of the angle formed by the hands on the clock and the other student uses a protractor to confirm the estimate. Then have students switch roles and practice for another five examples.

Use a Protractor to Measure an Angle in Degrees

Example

An angle is formed by two rays that share a common endpoint called the vertex. An angle's measure is between 0° and 180°. Use the following steps to find the measure of angle *DEF*.

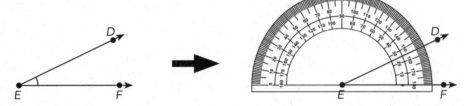

STEP 1 Place the base line of the protractor on ray *EF*.

STEP 2 Place the center of the base line of the protractor at the vertex of the angle, *E*.

STEP 3 Read the scale. Since ray *EF* crosses the 0 mark on the inner scale, read the angle measure from the inner scale. If *EF* crossed the 0 mark on the outer scale, you would read the angle measure from the outer scale.

Ray *ED* passes through the 25° mark. So, the measure of angle *DEF* is 25°.

✔ Quick Check

Measure ∠ *DEF*.

❶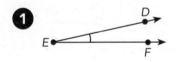

❷

❸

_____   _____   _____

Practice on Your Own
Measure ∠ *MOP*.

❹

❺

❻

_____   _____   _____

Use a Protractor to Draw Angles

TEACHING STRATEGY

1. **Vocabulary** Make sure students understand how to read and write names of angles. Point out that when you use three letters to name an angle, the vertex should always be the middle letter.

2. **Vocabulary** Direct students to the examples. If available, show students samples of different protractors. **Ask** On a protractor, what can help you line up the vertex correctly before finding the required measure? [Possible answer: a hole near the base line, a vertical line at the center of the base line] Demonstrate for students that a vertex may be placed anywhere on a line. The angle's arc will be the same for any vertex position as long as the vertex is lined up with the center of the base line on a protractor. For example, place three different vertices on a line and draw rays to measure 60° angles. Inform students that they may use either scale as they work through the Quick Check and Practice on Your Own exercises.

3. **Quick Check** Look for these common errors as students solve the quick check exercises.
   - Reading the inner scale of the protractor instead of the outer scale, or vice versa, yielding an angle that is the supplement of the correct angle.
   - Labeling the vertex with a letter other than the middle letter in the angle name.

4. **Next Steps** Assign the practice exercise to students who show understanding. For students who need more support, provide tutoring using the alternate teaching strategy.

Additional Teaching Resource

 Online Transition Guide with Reteach and Extra Practice worksheets from previous grade levels

ALTERNATE INTERVENTION STRATEGY

Materials: TRT50 (Clock), crayons, brads (or other fasteners), paper plate, scissors

Strategy: Use a model of a clock face to practice drawing angles.

1. Have students use crayons to shade the hour and minute hands, and then cut out all the pieces.

2. They should punch holes at the non-arrow ends for fastening to the paper plate.

3. Have students punch a hole in the center of their plate using a pencil. Insert a brad or other fastener through the clock hands, then through the plate, and secure.

4. Tell students that a full circle measures 360°. **Ask** Into how many sections do the numbers on a clock face divide a circle? [12] So, what is the measure of each of the 12 sections? [30°]

5. Name angles that are multiples of 30 and have students position the clock hands to form an angle of that measure. Accept all possible positions. For example, to model a 60-degree angle, students may place the hour hand at 1 and the minute hand at 3. After each example, have students follow the steps on the student page and use a protractor to draw the same angle.

6. Work through additional examples that are multiples of 15. Accept all possible positions. For example, for a 45-degree angle, students may place the hour hand halfway between 1 and 2 and the minute hand at 3. After each example, have students use a protractor to draw the same angle.

Use a Protractor to Draw Angles

Example 1 **Finding Unit Rates**

Draw angle *DEF* that measures 45°.

STEP 1 Draw line *GF* and label vertex *E*.

STEP 1 Place the base line of the protractor on line *GF*. Center the base line on vertex *E*.

STEP 1 On the inner scale of the protractor, 0° is on the right. Scan counterclockwise along the inner scale from 0° to 45°. Plot point *D*.

STEP 1 Remove the protractor. Draw a ray from vertex *E* through point *D*.

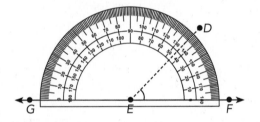

Example 2 **Comparing Unit Rates**

Draw angle *DEG* that measures 45°.

STEP 1 Draw line *GF* and label vertex *E*.

STEP 2 Place the base line of the protractor on line *GF*. Center the base line on vertex *E*.

STEP 3 On the outer scale of the protractor, 0° is on the left. Scan clockwise along the outer scale from 0° to 45°. Plot point *D*.

STEP 4 Remove the protractor. Draw a ray from vertex *E* through point *D*.

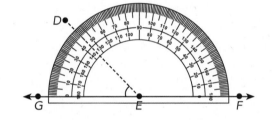

✓ Quick Check

Use a protractor to draw each angle.

1 m∠ABC = 75°

2 m∠FGH = 32°

Practice on Your Own
Use a protractor to draw each angle.

3 m∠JKL = 15°

4 m∠PQR = 120°

G
SKILL 39

Use a Protractor to Draw Perpendicular Line Segments

TEACHING STRATEGY

1. **Vocabulary** Make sure students understand the term *perpendicular*. Remind them that perpendicular lines intersect to form right angles.

2. **Teach** Direct students to the example. Ask What is the measure, in degrees, of a right angle? [90°] What measure should you always look for on a protractor to mark a perpendicular line? [90°] To help students understand perpendicular lines, have them name classroom objects with right angles. **Ask** What examples of right angles do you see in the classroom? [Possible answers: corners of rectangular walls, sheets of paper, index cards] Have students take a sheet of paper and line up its bottom left corner with the center of the base line of a protractor. Students should see that the left edge of the paper passes through the 90° mark on the protractor. Thus, the left and bottom edges of a sheet of paper are perpendicular.

3. **Quick Check** Look for this common error as students solve the Quick Check exercises.

   - Nonperpendicular lines being drawn because students have not aligned the given line with the base line of the protractor.

4. **Next Steps** Assign the practice exercises to students who show understanding. For students who need more support, provide tutoring using the alternate teaching strategy.

Additional Teaching Resource

 Online Transition Guide with Reteach and Extra Practice worksheets from previous grade levels

ALTERNATE INTERVENTION STRATEGY

Materials: protractors (or TRT17 Rulers/ Protractors)

Strategy: Use classroom items to familiarize students with perpendicular lines.

1. Hand out common classroom items with right angles, such as sheets of paper, index cards, or books.

2. In the center of a separate sheet of paper, ask students to trace the right edge and bottom edge of their item. Have them plot a point at the corner where the two lines meet. Tell students to use dashed lines to extend the vertical line down and the horizontal line to the right. (This may help them line up the protractor later in the activity.)

3. **Ask** What kind of angles are formed by the intersecting lines? [right angles] How many degrees should these angle measure? [90°] How can we best describe the intersection of these two lines? [They are perpendicular.]

4. Instruct students to place the protractor over their tracing. Tell them to place the base line of the protractor directly over one line so that the center of the base line is aligned with the point where the two lines they have traced intersect.

5. **Ask** Through what mark on the protractor does the other line pass? [90°] So, if you've aligned a line with the base line of a protractor and you want to draw a perpendicular, what mark on the protractor will that perpendicular pass through? [the 90° mark]

6. Have students repeat the process with a different right-angled object. Then have them again attempt to use a protractor to draw a perpendicular line segment.

Name _____ Date _____

Use a Protractor to Draw Perpendicular Line Segments

© Marshall Cavendish International (Singapore) Private Limited.

Example

STEP 1 Mark a point on line *XY* and label it *A*.

STEP 2 Place the base line of the protractor on line *XY*.

STEP 3 Align the center of the base line with point *A*.

STEP 4 Locate the 90° mark on the protractor. Plot point *B* at the 90° mark.

STEP 5 Align the straight edge of the protractor with points *A* and *B*. Draw a line connecting them. Line *AB* is perpendicular to line *XY*.

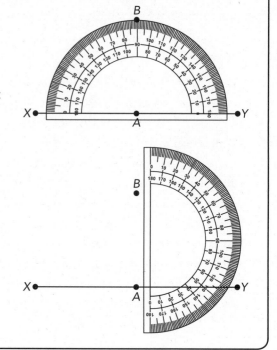

✔ Quick Check

Draw a line perpendicular to each line.

1

2

Practice on Your Own
Draw a line perpendicular to each line.

3

4

Apply Surface Area and Volume Formulas for Prisms

TEACHING STRATEGY

1. **Vocabulary** Make sure students understand the term *prism*. Remind them that a prism is a three-dimensional figure with two parallel polygon bases and rectangular faces that connect the two bases. A prism is named for the shape of its base—a *rectangular* prism has a *rectangular* base.

2. **Teach** Review with students the formulas for surface area and volume of a prism. You might want to identify the special formulas for the surface area and volume of a cube, a prism with sides of equal length: *S.A.* = $6s^2$ and *V* = s^3 (where s is the side length). Point out Example 1. **Ask** Do the front and back faces of the prism have the same dimensions? [Yes.] Do the left and right side faces have the same dimensions? [Yes.] And the top and bottom? [Yes.] Explain that this is why each of the products in the formula is multiplied by 2. Work through the example with students. Then have students look at Example 2. **Ask** Why is volume measured in cubic units? [Volume is calculated by multiplying three dimensions so it must be measured in cubic units.]

3. **Quick Check** Look for these common errors as students solve the Quick Check exercises.
   - Finding surface areas that are only half the correct value because students are finding the area of only one of each pair of faces/bases.
   - Not using square units for surface area and/or cubic units for volume.

Additional Teaching Resource

🖱 Online Transition Guide with Reteach and Extra Practice worksheets from previous grade levels

ALTERNATE INTERVENTION STRATEGY

Materials: connecting or unit cubes
Strategy: Use models to find the surface area and volume of rectangular prisms.

1. Hold up a connecting or unit cube and explain that it represents one cubic unit of volume.

2. Connect 12 cubes to form a 3-by-2-by-2 rectangular prism, as shown below. Have students count the number of cubes that make up the prism. **Ask** How many cubes are there in all? [12] How cubic units is the volume of the prism? [12 cubic units]

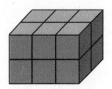

3. Review how to use the formula for volume of a prism (V = lwh). **Ask** Using the formula, what is the volume of the prism? [3 • 2 • 2 = 12 cubic units]

4. Now hold up the prism and have students sketch each of the 6 faces as you show them. Students should draw four 3-by-2 rectangles and two 2-by-2 squares. **Ask** What is the area of each rectangle? [6 square units] What is the area of each square? [4 square units] What is the sum of the areas of the six faces? [6 + 6 + 6 + 6 + 4 + 4 = 32 square units]

5. Review the formula for the surface area of a prism (S.A. = 2*lw* + 2*lh* + 2*wh*). Connect the formula to the work students did in Step 4. **Ask** Using the formula, what is the surface area of the prism? [32 square units]

6. Repeat the process with prisms of other dimensions until students are comfortable finding surface area and volume without the models.

Name _____ Date _____

Apply Surface Area and Volume Formulas for Prisms

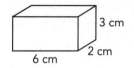

Example 1 Surface Area

Find the surface area of the prism.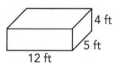

3 cm
2 cm
6 cm

STEP 1 Use the formula for the surface area of a rectangular prism.
S.A. = 2lw + 2lh + 2wh

STEP 2 Substitute values for the length l, width w, and height h.
S.A. = 2(6)(2) + 2(6)(3) + 2(2)(3)

STEP 3 Multiply, then add. Write the answer using square units.
S.A. = 24 + 36 + 12
S.A. = 72 cm²

The surface area of the prism is 72 cm².

Example 2 Volume

Find the volume of the prism.

4 ft
5 ft
12 ft

STEP 1 Use the formula for the volume of a rectangular prism.
V = lwh, or V = Bh (B = area of base)]

STEP 2 Substitute values for the length l, width w, and height h.
V = 12 • 5 • 4, or V = (12 • 5) • 4

STEP 3 Multiply. Write the answer using cubic units.
V = 240 ft³

The volume of the prism is 240 ft³.

✔ Quick Check

Find the surface area and volume of each prism.

1
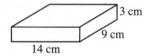
3 cm
9 cm
14 cm

S.A. = _____
V = _____

2

4 in.
4 in.
4 in.

S.A. = _____
V = _____

3
6 m
12 m
1.5 m

S.A. = _____
V = _____

Practice on Your Own
Find the surface area and volume of each prism.

4
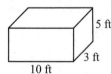
5 ft
3 ft
10 ft

S.A. = _____
V = _____

5
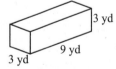
3 yd
9 yd
3 yd

S.A. = _____
V = _____

6
10 in.   10 in.
10 in.
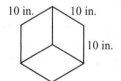

S.A. = _____
V = _____

Solve.

7 The volume of a prism is 324 m³. The prism has a square base and a height of 9 m. What is the length of each side of the base? _____

Find the Surface Area of a Square Pyramid

TEACHING STRATEGY	ALTERNATE INTERVENTION STRATEGY

TEACHING STRATEGY

1. **Vocabulary** Make sure students understand the term *square pyramid*. Remind them that a *pyramid* is a three-dimensional figure with a polygon base and triangular faces that meet at a common vertex. A pyramid is named for the shape of its base. For example, a square pyramid has a square base, while a triangular pyramid has a triangular base.

2. **Teach** Draw a square pyramid on the board or display a diagram of one. **Ask** How many sides are there in all? [5] What shape is the base? [a square] What shape is each of the faces? [a triangle] Do all the faces have the same dimensions? [Yes.] Have students look at the example and point out the formula. **Ask** In the formula, what is s^2? [the area of the square base] What is $\frac{1}{2}bh$? [the area of one triangular face] Why must you multiply $\frac{1}{2}bh$ by 4? [The pyramid has 4 triangular faces.] How could you rewrite the formula to replace $4(\frac{1}{2}bh)$? [Write $4(\frac{1}{2}bh)$ as $2bh$.] Work through the example with students, reminding them that they must write the units as square units.

3. **Quick Check** Look for these common errors as students solve the Quick Check exercises.
   • Adding the area of only one triangular face to the area of the base.
   • Forgetting to use square units in the answer.

4. **Next Steps** Assign the practice exercises to students who show understanding. For students who need more support, provide tutoring using the alternate teaching strategy.

Additional Teaching Resource

 Online Transition Guide with Reteach and Extra Practice worksheets from previous grade levels

ALTERNATE INTERVENTION STRATEGY

Materials: ruler, scissors, tape, TRT15 (Inch-Square Grid Paper)

Strategy: Use models to verify the formula for the surface area of a square pyramid.

1. Tell students that they are going to verify that the formula for finding the surface area of a pyramid is correct.

2. Instruct students to draw and cut out a square with sides measuring 5 inches on grid paper. Have students calculate the area of the square and write it on the square. [25 in.²]

3. Next, have students draw and cut out an isosceles triangle with a base of 5 inches and a height of 8 inches. Have students calculate the area of the triangle and write it on the triangle. [20 in.²]

4. Have students repeat Step 3 so that they have four congruent triangles.

5. Instruct students to find the sum of all five areas. [25 + 20 + 20 + 20 + 20 = 105 in.²]

6. Draw the following net on the board and instruct students to lay out their squares and triangles in the same way on their desks.

7. Have students tape together the bottom of each triangular face to the square base. Then, have them fold up the triangular faces and tape them together. **Ask** What kind of a figure do you have? [a square pyramid] Have students use the formula to confirm that 105 in.² is the surface area of the pyramid.

Name _____ Date _____

Find the Surface Area of a Square Pyramid

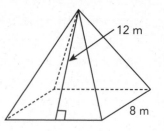

A pyramid has a square base measuring 8 m on each side. It has four faces that are congruent isosceles triangles. The height of each triangle is 12 m. What is the surface area of the square pyramid?

STEP 1 The surface area of a square pyramid is the sum of the area of the base and the areas of the 4 triangular faces.
You can use the formula:

$$S.A. = s^2 + 4(\tfrac{1}{2}bh)$$

STEP 2 Substitute values for the side, base, and height. $S.A. = (8)^2 + 4(\tfrac{1}{2})(8)(12)$

STEP 3 Multiply, then add. $S.A. = 64 + 192 = 256$

STEP 4 Write the answer using square units. $S.A. = 256 \text{ m}^2$

The surface area of the pyramid is 256 m².

 Quick Check

Find the surface area of each pyramid.

1 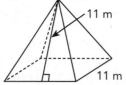 7 in.
10 in.

S.A. = _____

2 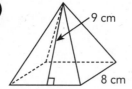 9 cm
8 cm

S.A. = _____

3  13 yd
12 yd

S.A. = _____

Practice on Your Own
Find the surface area of each pyramid.

4 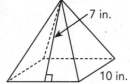 11 m
11 m

S.A. = _____

5 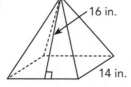 16 in.
14 in.

S.A. = _____

6 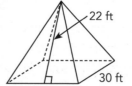 22 ft
30 ft

S.A. = _____

Solve.

7 A square pyramid has four faces that are congruent isosceles triangles. Find the surface area of the pyramid if the area of the base is 196 cm² and the height of each triangular face is 9 cm.

_____

Find the Area and Circumference of a Circle

G SKILL 42

TEACHING STRATEGY

1. **Vocabulary** Make sure students understand the terms *area* and *circumference*. Remind them that area is the number of square units needed to cover a surface, and circumference is the distance around a circle.

2. **Teach** Review with students the formulas for area and circumference of a circle. Draw a circle and label its radius and diameter. Note that the diameter is twice the radius. Point out Example 1. **Ask** What do you need to know to use the formula for the area of a circle? [radius] How do you find the radius of the wheel? [Divide the diameter by 2.] What do you do with the value for the radius? [Substitute 12 for *r*.] Then direct students' attention to Example 2. Point out that either formula may be used, depending on whether the radius or diameter is given. **Ask** Why is the circumference of the wheel an approximate measurement? [The value of π is approximately 3.14, so the answer is only an approximation and not exact.]

3. **Quick Check** Look for these common errors as students solve the Quick Check exercises.
   - Confusing the formulas for area and circumference.
   - Substituting the value for the diameter for *r* in the area formula.
   - Multiplying the radius by 2 instead of squaring when finding area.

4. **Next Steps** Assign the practice exercises to students who show understanding. For students who need more support, provide tutoring using the alternate teaching strategy.

Additional Teaching Resource

 Online Transition Guide with Reteach and Extra Practice worksheets from previous grade levels

ALTERNATE INTERVENTION STRATEGY

Materials: compass and ruler, TRT13 (Quarter-Inch Grid Paper)

Strategy: Estimate the area of a circle using circumscribed and inscribed squares.

1. Have students use a compass to draw a circle with a radius of 3 in. on the grid paper. Instruct them to label the center and draw a diameter inside the circle that is parallel to the bottom edge of their paper. **Ask** What is the length of the diameter? [6 in.]

2. Next, have students draw a square outside the circle, as shown below. **Ask** What is the side length of the square? Explain. [6 in.; each side of the square is the same length as the diameter of the circle.] Have students erase the diameter they drew in Step 1.

3. Finally, have students draw a square inside the circle, as shown below and one of its diagonals.

   Ask What is the length of the diagonal of the inner square? Explain. [6 in.; the diagonal is also the diameter of the circle.]

4. Use a ruler to estimate the length of the side of the smaller square. [about 4.25 in.]

5. Have students find the area of each square. [36 in.² and 18 in.²] **Ask** How does the area of the circle compare to the areas of the squares? [It is between the two.] Have students average the areas of the two squares. [36 + 18 = 54; 54 ÷ 2 = 27] Then work with students to find the area of the circle using the area formula and compare. [$A = \pi(3)^2 \approx 28.26$; 28.26 > 27]

Name _____ Date _____

Find the Area and Circumference of a Circle

Example

The wheels on Kim's bicycle have a diameter of 24 inches.

a) What is the area of one wheel?
Use 3.14 as an approximation for π.

STEP 1 Use the formula for the area of a circle:
$A = \pi r^2$ with r = radius.

Calculate the radius of the circle:
$r = 24 \div 2 = 12$ in.

STEP 2 Find the area of the wheel.
$A = \pi r^2$
$= \pi(12)^2$
$= \pi(144)$
$\approx 3.14 \bullet 144$
$= 452.16$

The area of the wheel is about 452.16 in.^{2}.

b) What is the circumference of one wheel?
Use 3.14 as an approximation for π.

Use the formula for the circumference of a circle:
$C = \pi d$ with d = diameter, or
$C = 2\pi r$ with r = radius.

$C = \pi(24)$
$\approx 3.14 \bullet 24$
$= 75.36$

The circumference of the wheel is about 75.36 in.

✓ Quick Check
Solve. Use 3.14 as an approximation for π.

1 A circle has a radius of 30 cm.

a) What is the area of the circle? _____

b) What is the circumference of the circle? _____

2 A circle has a diameter of 4 ft.

a) What is the area of the circle? _____

b) What is the circumference of the circle? _____

Practice on Your Own
Solve. Use 3.14 as an approximation for π.

3 A circle has a diameter of 22 in.

a) What is the area of the circle? _____

b) What is the circumference of the circle? _____

4 A circle has a radius of 8 m.

a) What is the area of the circle? _____

b) What is the circumference of the circle? _____

G
SKILL 43 # Identify Nets of Prisms and Pyramids

TEACHING STRATEGY

1. **Vocabulary** Make sure students understand the term *net*. Explain that a *net* is a two-dimensional diagram of the bases and faces of a three-dimensional figure. A net is arranged in such a way that the diagram can be folded to form the three-dimensional figure.

2. **Teach** Tell students that when they examine a net, they should pay attention to the number of bases and faces to help them identify the solid formed by the net. Have students examine the examples. **Ask** How many bases/faces does a cube have? [6] What is the shape of each? [a square] How many bases/faces does a rectangular prism have? [6] Have student identify the pairs of congruent rectangles in Example 2. Explain that in the rectangular prism that is formed, these are top-and-bottom, left-and-right, front-and-back faces. **Ask** How many bases does a triangular prism have? [2] How many faces? [3] Which of the three-dimensional figures has only one base? [pyramid] Why must the net for a square pyramid have 4 triangular faces? [A square pyramid's faces are made up of triangles. This pyramid has a square base, which means there always must be 4 triangular faces.]

3. **Quick Check** Look for these common errors as students solve the Quick Check exercises.
   • Confusing nets of square pyramids and triangular prisms because they both include triangles and rectangles.
   • Forgetting that the dashed lines on a net indicate where to fold the diagram.

Additional Teaching Resource

 Online Transition Guide with Reteach and Extra Practice worksheets from previous grade levels

ALTERNATE INTERVENTION STRATEGY

Materials: TRT51–54 (Nets) scissors, tape

Strategy: Construct solids from nets.

1. Hand out the nets to students. Tell them that they are going to construct solids from nets.

2. Instruct students to cut out the first net (for a cube). Explain that the dotted lines indicate where to fold the net. Work with students to fold the net and tape the edges together. **Ask** How many bases/faces does this figure have? [6] What is the shape of each? [a square] What solid is formed? [a cube] On the board, begin a chart with the headings *Solid, Number of Bases/Faces, Shape of Base(s)*, and *Shape of Faces*. In the first row, record the information for a cube.

3. Next, have students cut out the net for a rectangular prism, fold on the dotted lines, and tape the edges together. Instruct students to record the information for a rectangular prism in the second row of the chart.

4. Continue the process for the last two nets. Complete the chart with the information for triangular prisms and square pyramids.

5. Have students compare and contrast the solids they created. **Ask** How are a cube and a square pyramid alike and different? [They both have square bases, but the cube has two bases and the pyramid has only one. The faces of a cube are squares, but the faces of a pyramid are triangles.] How are a triangular prism and a square pyramid alike and different? [They are made up of the same shapes. In the prism the triangles are bases, but in the pyramid a square is the base. The pyramid has four triangles and one square, while the prism has two triangles and three rectangles.]

Identify Nets of Prisms and Pyramids

Example 1 Cube

This net shows six congruent squares. It can be folded to form a square prism, also called a cube.

This is a net of a cube.

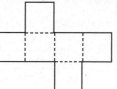

Example 2 Rectangular Prism

This net shows three pairs of congruent rectangles. Any pair can be considered the bases of the prism.

This is a net of a rectangular prism.

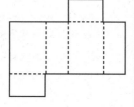

Example 3 Triangular Prism

This net shows two congruent triangles (parallel bases) and three rectangles (faces).

This is a net of a triangular prism.

Example 4 Square Pyramid

This net shows a square base and four faces that are congruent triangles.

This is a net of a square pyramid.

 Quick Check

Classify each triangle by its side lengths.

1

_____

2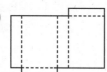

_____

3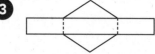

_____

Practice on Your Own
Classify each triangle by its side lengths.

4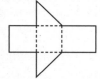

_____

5

_____

6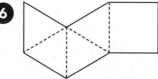

_____

Classify the triangle described below.

7 The net for a solid has 6 faces. None of the faces are squares or triangles.

What solid does this net form? _____

Find the Mean of a Set of Data

TEACHING STRATEGY

1. **Vocabulary** Point out that *mean* has several different meanings in everyday speech. Tell students that, in mathematics, *mean* has one meaning: The mean of a set of values is the sum of the values divided by the number of values. Point out that we often refer to the mean as the *average*.

2. **Teach** Direct students to Example 1. Tell students that the numbers form a data set. Each number is a **value**. **Ask** How do you find the sum of the values? [Add them.] How many data values are there? [5] Tell students that even if a value is 0, it must be counted as part of the data set. **Ask** Once you find the sum of the values and you have counted the number of values, how do you find the mean? [Divide the sum of the values by the number of values.] Direct students to Example 2.
   Ask What are you being asked to find? [the mean of the long jump distances] Review each step with the students again. Tell students that the mean distance jumped is the same as the average distance jumped. **Ask** What are some measurements for which means are often calculated? [Possible answers: weather data, sports statistics, test scores]

3. **Quick Check** Look for this common error as students solve the Quick Check exercises.
   • Some students may have trouble with decimal computation.

4. **Next Steps** Assign the practice exercises to students who show understanding. For students who need more support, provide tutoring using the alternate teaching strategy.

Additional Teaching Resource
 Online Transition Guide with Reteach and Extra Practice worksheets from previous grade levels

ALTERNATE INTERVENTION STRATEGY

Materials: none

Strategy: Gather data values to create a data set and find the mean.

1. Tell students that they will be working in groups to gather data, record it, and then find the mean of the data set. Help students form groups of at least four students.

2. Ask each group to survey its members to find out the total number of brothers and sisters each student has.

3. As members of a group give their responses, everyone in the group should record the data, listing the names of all the members of the group and, next to each name, the number of siblings that student has.

4. When each group has finished surveying its members, tell group members that they have just created a data set, and that each number in the set is a value.

5. Ask What is the first step in finding the mean of a set of values? [Find the sum of the values.] Have students find the sum. **Ask** What is the second step in finding the mean of a set of values? [Count the number of values in the set.] Have students count the values. **Ask** What is the final step in finding the mean of a set of values? [Divide the sum of the values by the number of values.] Have students divide.
   Ask Can the mean be a decimal number, while the data values must be whole numbers? [Yes] Have students round the mean to two decimal places if necessary.

6. Have a volunteer from each group share the result with the rest of the class.

7. If time allows, have students follow the same process to find the mean number of household pets for each group.

Find the Mean of a Set of Data

The mean is one measure of the center of a data set.
To find the mean of a data set, follow these steps.

STEP 1   Find the sum of the values in the data set.

STEP 2   Count the number of values in the data set.

STEP 3   Divide the sum of the values in the data set by the number of values.

Example 1

Find the mean of 9, 16, 28, 43, and 34.

STEP 1   Find the sum of the values.
$$9 + 16 + 28 + 43 + 34 = 130$$

STEP 2   Count the number of values.
There are 5 values in the data set.

STEP 3   Divide the sum by the number of values.
$$\frac{130}{5} = 26$$

The mean of the data set is 26.

Example 2

The distances, in feet, of long jumps are below.
11.2, 13.7, 16.8, 14.5, 17.3, 13.5
Find the mean distance jumped.

STEP 1   Find the sum of the distances.
$$11.2 + 13.7 + 16.8 + 14.5 + 17.3 + 13.5$$
$$= 87 \text{ ft}$$

STEP 2   Count the number of jumps.
There are 6 jumps.

STEP 3   Divide the sum of the distances by the number of jumps.
$$\frac{87}{6} = 14.5$$

The mean distance jumped is 14.5 feet.

✔ Quick Check

Find the mean of each set of data.
Round your answer to two decimal places if it is not exact.

1 3, 67, 72, 6

2 2, 9, 15, 18, 23

3 32, 5.7, 14, 3, 16.5

_____   _____   _____

Practice on Your Own
Solve. Show your work.
Round your answer to two decimal places if it is not exact.

4 The speeds, in miles per hour, of 8 cars are shown below.

   50, 47, 49, 55, 45, 42, 53, 36

   Find the mean speed of the cars. _____

5 The weights, in pounds, of 9 dogs are shown below.

   45, 17.25, 72, 65.3, 23, 15, 30.67, 12.5, 87

   Find the mean weight of the dogs. _____

Find the Median of a Set of Data

TEACHING STRATEGY

1. **Vocabulary** Tell students that another way to say *median* is "middle value." Review the mathematical meaning of *mean* and make sure students understand the difference between the two terms.

2. **Teach** Direct students to Example 1. **Ask** What must you first do to find the middle value in a data set? [Order all the values from least to greatest.] Tell students to be careful when ordering a data set to always include every piece of data. Stress that repeated values must be included. **Ask** How many values are in this set? [5] What is the middle value? [29] What is the median? [29] Point out that when a data set includes an odd number of values, there is always a single middle value. Direct students to Example 2. **Ask** How many values are in this set? [6] Tell students that when a data set has an even number of values, there are two values in the middle. Explain that to find the median in such cases, they must calculate the mean of the two middle values. **Ask** How do you find the mean of two numbers? [Add the numbers, then divide by 2.]

3. **Quick Check** Look for these common errors as students solve the Quick Check exercises.
   - Ordering the values incorrectly.
   - When finding the mean of two middle values, dividing their sum by the total number of values in the set.

4. **Next Steps** Assign the practice exercises. For students who need more support, provide tutoring using the alternate teaching strategy.

Additional Teaching Resource

 Online Transition Guide with Reteach and Extra Practice worksheets from previous grade levels

ALTERNATE INTERVENTION STRATEGY

Materials: index cards

Strategy: Use manipulatives to represent a data set and find its median.

1. Write the following list of 7 values on the board, and have students copy each value onto an index card.

   6 14 3 65 56 3 40

2. **Ask** Are any values in the set repeated? [Yes, 3 appears twice.] Have students place the cards on a desk, in order from least to greatest. Write the ordered set on the board.

   3 3 6 14 40 56 65

3. **Ask** How many values are in the set? [7] What is the middle value in the set? [14] What is the median? [14]

4. Repeat Steps 1 and 2 with the following list of values: 8, 6, 9, 11, 5, 13, 0, 9. Make sure students include both the second 9 and the zero in their set of cards.

5. **Ask** How many values are in the set? [8] Explain that when there is an even number of values in a data set, there is no single middle value. **Ask** What are the two middle values in the set? [8 and 9]

6. Tell students that when a set has an even number of values, the median is the mean of the two middle values. **Ask** How can you find the median of 8 and 9? [Add the two values, and divide the sum by 2.] Have a volunteer demonstrate the calculation on the board. **Ask** What is the mean of the two middle values in this data set? [8.5] Is this median one of the values in the set? [No]

7. Give students several other data sets, with both even and odd numbers of values, and have them repeat the process on their own.

SP
SKILL 45 # Find the Median of a Set of Data

Example 1	**Odd Number of Values**

Find the median of the values 32, 27, 52, 3, and 29.

STEP 1 Write the values from least to greatest.

3 27 29 32 52

STEP 2 Count to identify the middle value. There are two values less than 29 and two values greater than 29. So, 29 is the middle value.

3 27 (29) 32 52

The median is 29.

Example 2	**Even Number of Values**

Find the median of the values 66, 33, 34, 78, 9, and 15.

STEP 1 Write the values from least to greatest.

9 15 33 34 66 78

STEP 2 Count to identify the middle value.

9 15 (33 34) 66 78

Since the number of values is an even number (6), there are two middle values, 33 and 34.

STEP 3 Find the mean of the two middle values.

$$\frac{33 + 34}{2} = \frac{67}{2} = 33.5$$

The median is 33.5.

✔ Quick Check

Find the median of each set of numbers.

1 98, 102, 56, 45, 99

_____

2 1, 13, 3, 64, 51, 79

_____

3 2, 5, 2, 1, 13, 6, 7, 12, 9, 0, 10

_____

4 334, 434, 333, 443, 343, 444, 433, 443

_____

Practice on Your Own
Solve. Show your work.

5 The weekly rainfall, in inches, for the past 7 weeks is shown below.

2, 1.8, 1, 0.5, 0, 2, 1.5

What was the median rainfall? _____

6 A student's spelling test scores are shown below.

76, 83, 62, 85, 92, 51, 71, 78, 100, 88, 95, 78

What was the median test score? _____

Draw Frequency Tables and Dot Plots

TEACHING STRATEGY

1. **Vocabulary** Tell students that the term frequency describes "how often" something happens. **Ask** If a car breaks down frequently, how often does it break down? [very often] Explain that a frequency table lists values in a data set and shows how often each value appears.

2. **Teach** Direct students to the data set in the example. **Ask** How many values are in the data set? [16] What is the least value? [1] The greatest? [9] What range of values is shown in the top row of the frequency table? [1 to 9] How many times does the value 6 appear in the data set? [once] Show students that this is represented in the table by the 1 in the cell immediately below the 6 in the top row. Use this process for every value in the top row. **Ask** How is the table of organized data helpful? [The table makes it easier to analyze the data.] How many students rehearsed for 8 hours? [0] What is the longest amount of time anyone spent rehearsing? [9 hours] Review the parts of the dot plot. **Ask** How many students rehearsed for 5 hours? [2] For 4 hours? [3]

3. **Quick Check** Look for these common errors as students solve the Quick Check exercises.
   - Leaving values that do not appear in the data set out of the frequency table or dot plot, because students don't recognize that they must show the full range of data.

4. **Next Steps** Assign the practice exercises to students who show understanding. For students who need more support, provide tutoring using the alternate teaching strategy.

Additional Teaching Resource
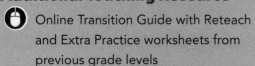 Online Transition Guide with Reteach and Extra Practice worksheets from previous grade levels

ALTERNATE INTERVENTION STRATEGY

Materials: index cards

Strategy: Write data points on index cards to more easily organize data into frequency tables and dot plots.

1. List the following numbers on the board: 51, 51, 56, 58, 55, 51, 52, 54, 52, 54, 52, 53, 52, 53, 52, 54, 52, 56, 51, 55. Have students copy the list onto a sheet of paper. Tell students that the numbers represent a swimmer's times, in seconds, in 20 races.

2. Give each pair of students a stack of 20 index cards. Have students copy each of the values onto a separate card, crossing off a data value in the set as they copy it.

3. **Ask** students to sort the cards into separate piles by value and to order the values from least to greatest. Have students fan each pile of cards into a vertical column.

4. Tell students that they have just organized a data set in a way that will help them to analyze the data. **Ask** What is the least value? [51] The greatest? [58] What is the range of values for the swimmer's times? [51 to 58 seconds]

5. Help students organize the data into a table. Draw a two-row table with nine columns on the board. In the top left cell, write "Time in Seconds". In the bottom left cell, write "Number of Races". **Ask** What values should appear in the top row? [51 to 58] Have students write numbers in the top row. **Ask** In how many races did the swimmer finish in 51 seconds? [4] Write that value in the cell under 51. Continue through the other values to complete the data table.

6. Step students through the creation of a dot plot for the data set. Relate both the frequency table and the dot plot to the arrangement of index cards students created.

Name _____ Date _____

Draw Frequency Tables and Dot Plots

Example

The box below contains a data set.

The values give the number of hours each of 16 students spent rehearsing for a play.

3	7	5	6	4	5	7	7
2	4	7	1	2	9	3	4

The data can be summarized in a frequency table.

A frequency table shows how many times each value in a data set appears.

This data set includes values from 1 to 9. These values are shown in the top row of the table.

The bottom row shows the frequency, how many times each value appears in the data set.

Number of Hours Rehearsing	1	2	3	4	5	6	7	8	9
Number of Students	1	2	2	3	2	1	4	0	1

This data set also can be displayed in a dot plot.

The number line shows the range of values that appear in the data set: 1 to 9.

The number of dots above each number shows how many times that value appears in the data set.

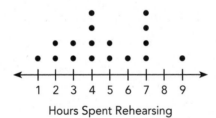

Hours Spent Rehearsing

✓ Quick Check
Summarize the data set in a frequency table and draw a dot plot.

1 The data show the number of vacation days 12 workers have taken this year.

6	9	0	6	5	6	6	4	5	5	6	8

Practice on Your Own
Summarize the data set in a frequency table and draw a dot plot.

2 The data show the number of paintings created by 20 students in a summer painting class.

5	8	4	6	9	2	3	12	5	4
4	6	2	2	6	5	4	3	5	8

Express Part of a Whole as a Fraction and a Percent

RP
SKILL 47

TEACHING STRATEGY

1. **Vocabulary** Make sure students understand the terms *numerator*, *denominator*, and *percent*. Remind them that the denominator (bottom number) of a fraction shows the total number of equal parts a whole is divided into, and the numerator (top number) shows how many parts are present. A percent is a way of expressing a fraction with a denominator of 100. Tell students that the term *percent* comes from the Latin *per cent*, which means "per hundred."

2. **Teach** Direct students to Step 1 of the example. **Ask** What information in the problem indicates a part-whole model? [You are asked to express 6 books out of 15 books] Into how many equal parts should the whole bar be divided? [15] What will each part represent? [1 book] How many parts will represent 6 books? [6] What will be the denominator of your fraction? [15] The numerator? [6] Remind students that the numerator and denominator of a fraction in simplest form have no common factors other than 1. **Ask** What are the factors of 6? [1, 2, 3, 6] What are the factors of 15? [1, 3, 5, 15] Do 6 and 15 share a factor besides 1? [Yes, 3.] To express $\frac{6}{15}$ in simplest form, what do you need to do? [Divide the numerator and denominator by the common factor, 3.] What is $\frac{6}{15}$ in simplest form? [$\frac{2}{5}$] Point out to students that in order to express a fraction in simplest form they need to divide the numerator and denominator by their greatest common factor (GCF).

Ask What are the common factors of 16 and 24? [2, 4, 8] What is the GCF? [8] What is $\frac{16}{24}$ in simplest form? [$\frac{2}{3}$]

Direct students to Step 2 of the Example. Remind students that to write an equivalent fraction, they must multiply or divide the numerator and denominator by the same number. **Ask** When finding a percent, what are you being asked to find? [an equivalent fraction with 100 as the denominator] What factor do you multiply by 5 to get 100? [20] To find an equivalent fraction for $\frac{2}{5}$ with a denominator of 100, by what number do you multiply the numerator? [20] Tell students that they can check equivalent fractions using cross multiplication.

Direct students to Step 3 of the Example.

Ask What is another way to find the percent of remaining books? [Write the remaining books as a fraction: $\frac{9}{15} = \frac{3}{5} = \frac{60}{100} = 60\%$]

3. **Quick Check** Look for these common errors as students solve the Quick Check exercises.
   - Incorrectly writing fractions, indicating confusion between numerators and denominators.
   - Not expressing fractions in simplest from, indicating either a failure to recognize simplest form or a failure to recognize common factors.
   - Miscalculating percent, demonstrating a lack of understanding regarding equivalent fractions.

4. **Next Steps** Assign the practice exercises to students who show understanding.

Additional Teaching Resource

 Online Transition Guide with Reteach and Extra Practice worksheets from previous grade levels

RP
SKILL 47

Express Part of a Whole as a Fraction and a Percent

Example

Charlie places 15 books on a shelf. Six of them are math books. Express 6 books out of 15 books as a fraction and as a percent.

STEP 1 Draw a model to represent the fraction. Write the fraction in simplest form.

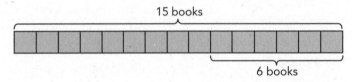

15 books

6 books

$\frac{6}{15} = \frac{2}{5}$ So, 6 books out of 15 books can be expressed as the fraction $\frac{2}{5}$.

STEP 2 Express the fraction as a percent. First rewrite $\frac{2}{5}$ as an equivalent fraction with 100 as the denominator.

$\frac{2}{5} = \frac{2 \cdot 20}{5 \cdot 20} = \frac{40}{100} = 40\%$

STEP 3 Express the remaining 9 books out of 15 books as a percent.
Subtract 40% from 100%: 100% − 40% = 60%.
So, 9 books out of 15 books can be expressed as 60%.

✓ Quick Check
Solve.

1 Express 15 goldfish out of 60 goldfish as a fraction in simplest form.

_____

2 If there are 21 dogs in a group of 30 animals, what percent of the animals are dogs?

_____

Practice on Your Own
Solve.

3 There are 28 violinists in an orchestra of 100 musicians. What percent of the musicians in the orchestra are violinists?

_____

4 Express 40 sandwiches out of 50 sandwiches as a fraction in simplest form.

_____

5 18 out of 54 coins are dimes. What fraction of the coins are dimes? Write your answer in simplest form.

_____

6 48 out of 150 flowers are roses. What percent of the flowers are not roses?

_____

Express a Fraction as a Percent

TEACHING STRATEGY

1. **Vocabulary** Explain the difference between proper fractions and improper fractions. In a proper fraction, the numerator (top number) is less than the denominator (bottom number). In an improper fraction, the numerator is greater than the denominator. When you write an improper fraction as a percent, it is greater than 100%.

2. **Teach** Tell students that fractions and percents are different ways to express "parts" of numbers. **Ask** If I drink an entire bottle of water, I will I have drunk 100% of the water. If I drink just a half bottle, what percent of the water will I have drunk? [50%] Direct students to Example 1. **Ask** How do you express a fraction as a percent? [First multiply the fraction by 100%, then divide the numerator by the denominator.] Point out that just as the fraction represents 2 parts out of 7, the percent represents 28.57 parts out of 100. Direct students to Example 2. **Ask** What type of fraction has a percent that is greater than 100%? [improper]

3. **Quick Check** Look for these common errors as students solve the Quick Check exercises.
   - Incorrectly placing the decimal point in the percent, indicating that the student has divided the fraction by 100% instead of multiplying.
   - Faulty rounding.

4. **Next Steps** Assign the practice exercises to students who show understanding. For students who need more support, provide tutoring using the alternate teaching strategy.

Additional Teaching Resource

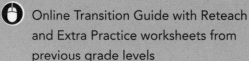 Online Transition Guide with Reteach and Extra Practice worksheets from previous grade levels

ALTERNATE INTERVENTION STRATEGY

Materials: none

Strategy: Use proportions to write fractions as percents.

1. Explain to students that percent means "per hundred". So you can write a percent as the ratio of a number compared to 100.

2. Remind students that a proportion is a statement that two ratios are equal. Give the following example:

$$\frac{3}{5} = \frac{60}{100}$$

3. Point out that $\frac{60}{100}$ can be read as "60 per 100," or in other words, "60 percent." **Ask** What proportion would you set up to write $\frac{13}{50}$ as a percent? [$\frac{13}{50} = \frac{?}{100}$]

4. To solve the proportion, set up the following statement: $\frac{13 \times \square}{50 \times \square} = \frac{\square}{100}$. **Ask** What number do you need to multiply 50 by to get 100? [2] If you multiply the bottom number of the fraction by 2, what must you do to the top number? [Multiply by 2.] Explain that since $13 \times 2 = 26$, the "per hundred" fraction is $\frac{26}{100}$. Ask What is $\frac{13}{50}$ expressed as a percent? [26%]

5. Have students work in groups to repeat the process using the following examples: $\frac{1}{5}, \frac{11}{20}, \frac{14}{25}, \frac{9}{50}$. [20%, 55%, 56%, 18%] Students should write a proportion for each example and solve using the process modeled above. Remind students to add the % symbol to the final answer.

RP

SKILL 48 # Express a Fraction as a Percent

Example 1 **Proper Fraction** ────

Express $\frac{2}{7}$ as a percent. Round your answer to 2 decimal places.

$\frac{2}{7} \times 100\%$ Multiply the fraction by 100%.

$= \frac{200}{7}\%$ Divide the numerator by the denominator: $200 \div 7$.

$= 28.57\%$ Round the answer to 2 decimal places.

Example 2 **Improper Fraction** ────

Express $\frac{11}{4}$ as a percent. Round your answer to 2 decimal places.

$\frac{11}{4} \times 100\%$ Multiply the fraction by 100%.

$= \frac{1,100}{4}\%$ Divide the numerator by the denominator: $1,100 \div 4$.

$= 275\%$

✓ Quick Check

Write each fraction as a percent. Round your answer to 2 decimal places if necessary.

1 $\frac{4}{5}$

2 $\frac{1}{9}$

3 $\frac{10}{8}$

_____   _____   _____

Practice on Your Own

Write each fraction as a percent. Round your answer to 2 decimal places if necessary.

4 $\frac{12}{25}$

5 $\frac{25}{12}$

6 $\frac{85}{50}$

_____   _____   _____

7 $\frac{6}{8}$

8 $\frac{9}{7}$

9 $\frac{4}{12}$

_____   _____   _____

10 $\frac{9}{36}$

11 $\frac{2}{3}$

12 $\frac{12}{5}$

_____   _____   _____

Express a Percent as a Fraction or Decimal

TEACHING STRATEGY

1. **Vocabulary** Review with students the meanings of *percent* and *decimal*. Remind students that *percent* literally means "per hundred," and the root "deci–" in decimal refers to the number 10. Decimal places in numbers represent multiples of 10.

2. **Teach** Direct students to Example 1. **Ask** How do you express a percent as a fraction? [Write the percent as a fraction with a denominator of 100.] Tell students that when the numerator is not a whole number (i.e. when it is a decimal), they must first multiply the numerator and the denominator by a multiple of 10 to express both digits as whole numbers. For example, $1.2\% = \frac{1.2}{100} = \frac{1.2 \times 10}{100 \times 10} = \frac{12}{1000} = \frac{3}{250}$. Direct students to Example 2. **Ask** How do you express a percent as a decimal? [Divide the number by 100 and drop the % symbol.]

3. **Quick Check** Look for these common errors as students solve the Quick Check exercises.
   - Not expressing fractions in simplest form due to an inability to recognize common factors.
   - Incorrectly expressing fractions in simplest form, possibly due to a failure to divide both the numerator and denominator by the same factor.
   - Incorrect placement of decimal points.

4. **Next Steps** Assign the practice exercises to students who show understanding. For students who need more support, provide tutoring using the alternate teaching strategy.

Additional Teaching Resource

 Online Transition Guide with Reteach and Extra Practice worksheets from previous grade levels

ALTERNATE INTERVENTION STRATEGY

Materials: none

Strategy: Use knowledge of decimal places to express percents as decimals.

1. Help students understand the relationship between a percent and a decimal. Tell students that 100% expressed as a decimal is 1.0. Any percent greater than 100% will be a decimal number greater than 1. And any percent less than 100% will be a decimal number less than 1.

2. Tell students that another strategy for expressing a percent as a decimal is to divide by 100 using decimal places. First, if a percent does not include a decimal point, place one after the final digit. Then move the decimal point two places to the left. Model the strategy using 25% as an example:

$$25\% = 2\underbrace{5.}_{} = 0.25$$

3. Explain to students that moving a decimal point two places to the left is the same as dividing by 100. Point out that a decimal expression of a percent will always be less than the percent because it is divided by 100.

4. Repeat the strategy using 1-digit and 3-digit percent numbers. For 1-digit percents, such as 4%, model writing 3 zeros before the number to ensure correct placement of the decimal point. (4% = 0.004) With 3-digit percents, such as 235%, point out that the decimal number will always be 1 or greater. (235% = 2.35)

5. Revisit the Quick Check exercises and have students express items 4–6 as decimals using the alternate strategy. Remind students to move the decimal point to the left when writing a percent as a decimal.

RP
SKILL 49

Express a Percent as a Fraction or Decimal

Example 1   Percent as Fraction

Express 52% as a fraction in simplest form.

$52\% = \dfrac{52}{100}$ Express the percent as a fraction with a denominator of 100.

$\quad = \dfrac{52 \div 4}{100 \div 4}$ Divide both the numerator and the denominator by 4, their greatest common factor.

$\quad = \dfrac{13}{25}$

Example 2   Percent as Decimal

Express 132% as a decimal.

$132\% = \dfrac{132}{100}$ Express the percent as a fraction with a denominator of 100.

$\quad = 1.32$ Divide 132 by 100 to express the fraction as a decimal.

✔ Quick Check

Write each percent as a fraction or a mixed number in simplest form.

1 76%

2 21%

3 124%

_____

_____

_____

Write each percent as a decimal.

4 299%

5 42.3%

6 8%

_____

_____

_____

Practice on Your Own

Write each percent as a fraction or a mixed number in simplest form.

7 148%

8 2.6%

9 65%

_____

_____

_____

Write each percent as a decimal.

10 413%

11 9.3%

12 0.1%

_____

_____

_____

Express a Ratio as a Fraction or Percent

TEACHING STRATEGY

1. **Vocabulary** Make sure students understand the terms *ratio*, *fraction*, and *percent*. A ratio is a comparison of two or more numbers, called the *terms* of the ratio. A *fraction* is a number that names part of a whole or part of a group. In a fraction, the *numerator* names the part and the *denominator* names the whole. *Percent* means "per hundred." It is a ratio of a number to 100.

2. **Teach** Explain to students that ratios, fractions, and percents are related because they are all examples of number comparisons. Ratios can express part-to-part or part-to-whole comparisons. Fractions are ratios that express part-to-whole comparisons. Percents are also ratios that express part-to-whole comparisons. For example, a flower arrangement is made up of 6 lilies and 9 tulips. The ratio of lilies to tulips can be written as 6 to 9, 6 : 9, or $\frac{6}{9}$. If the flower arrangement contains 15 flowers total (6 lilies + 9 tulips = 15 flowers), then the fraction of flowers that are tulips can be written as $\frac{9}{15}$, or as $\frac{3}{5}$ in simplest form. The percent of flowers that are tulips can be written as 60%.

   Review part (a) of the Example with students. **Ask** What do each of the squares in the models represent? [Each square represents 1 student.] In Step 2, why do you need to find the total number of students in order to write the fraction? [A fraction compares a part to a whole. You need to know the total number of students in order to write the denominator.]

Ask In Step 3, what must you do first to simplify the fraction? [You must find the greatest common factor (GCF) of 9 and 24.] If necessary, guide students through the steps to finding the GCF of 9 and 24. **Ask** What are the factors of 9? [1, 3, and 9] What are the factors of 24? [1, 2, 3, 4, 6, 8, 12, and 24] What is the GCF of 9 and 24? [3]

Review part (b) of the Example with students. **Ask** In Step 1, why do you multiply the fraction $\frac{3}{8}$ by 100? [Percent means "per hundred." To find the percent, you must multiply by 100%.] Point out Step 2. Tell students that it is easier to round percents by converting the fraction to a decimal and not a mixed number. If necessary, review the rules for rounding a decimal to the nearest ones place. **Ask** Why is it appropriate to say that *about* 38% of the class are boys? [You have rounded 37.5% to 38%, so using the word *about* shows that the number is an approximation, not an exact answer.]

3. **Quick Check** Look for these common errors as students solve the Quick Check exercises.
   - Writing the terms of a ratio in the incorrect order, showing a lack of understanding of the concept.
   - Expressing a fraction as a number of parts to a number of parts, rather than a number of parts to the whole.
   - Incorrectly simplifying fractions by dividing the numerator and denominator by different factors or using a common factor but not the GCF.
   - Making computational errors when converting a fraction to a percent.

4. **Next Steps** Assign the practice exercises to students who show understanding.

Additional Teaching Resource

 Online Transition Guide with Reteach and Extra Practice worksheets from previous grade levels

Express a Ratio as a Fraction or Percent

Example

In Ms. Bendel's class, the ratio of boys to girls is 9 to 15.

a) What fraction of the class are boys? Write the fraction in simplest form.

STEP 1 Draw a model. Each unit in the model should represent one student.

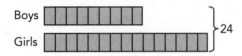

Boys
Girls
} 24

STEP 2 Find the total number of students: 24. There are 9 boys. So the numerator is 9 and the denominator is 24 : $\frac{9}{24}$.

STEP 3 The greatest common factor of 9 and 24 is 3. Divide the numerator and denominator by 3.

$$\frac{9}{24} = \frac{9 \div 3}{24 \div 3} = \frac{3}{8}$$

The fraction of the class that are boys is $\frac{3}{8}$.

b) What percent of the class are boys? Round your answer to the nearest whole percent.

STEP 1 Multiply the fraction of students that are boys by 100%.

$$\frac{3}{8} \times 100\% = \frac{300}{8}\%$$

STEP 2 Divide the numerator by the denominator.

$$\frac{300}{8}\% = 37.5\%$$

STEP 3 Round.

37.5% rounds up to 38%

About 38% of the class are boys.

✔ Quick Check
Solve. Write the fraction in simplest form. Round the percent to the nearest whole percent.

1 A pet store has 4 kittens and 6 puppies available for adoption.

a) What fraction of the pets available for adoption are kittens? _____

b) What percent of the pets available for adoption are kittens? _____

Practice on Your Own
Solve. Write the fraction in simplest form. Round the percent to the nearest whole percent.

2 In a recent survey, people were asked their preferred flavor of ice cream, among chocolate, strawberry, and vanilla. Here are the results: 32 people chose chocolate, 18 people chose strawberry, and 30 people chose vanilla.

a) What fraction of people chose strawberry as their preferred flavor? _____

b) What percent of people chose strawberry as their preferred flavor? _____

Solve a Histogram Problem

TEACHING STRATEGY

1. **Vocabulary** Make sure students understand the term *histogram*. Remind them that a histogram does not show individual data points. Instead it shows the frequency of data within equal ranges of values. Point out that the bars are all drawn next to each other because the data is continuous. No data points fall between the bars.

2. **Teach** Direct students to the Example. **Ask** What information will go on the *x*-axis of your histogram? [the age intervals] The *y*-axis? [the number of people in each age range] Explain that the greatest value on the scale for the *y*-axis should be at least as great as the greatest frequency in the table. **Ask** What is the greatest frequency in the table? [18] In part (c), what information do you need to write the fraction for the people who are over 40? [You need to find the number of people over 40 (the numerator) and the total number of people (the denominator).] Why must you multiply the fraction by 100 to find the percent? [Percent is a ratio of a number to 100.]

3. **Quick Check** Look for these common errors as students solve the Quick Check exercises.
   • Not drawing bars adjacent to each other.
   • Specifying ranges that are not all equal in size or that leave out data points.
     These errors show a lack of understanding of the unique qualities of a histogram.

4. **Next Steps** Assign the practice exercises. For students who need more support, provide tutoring using the alternate teaching strategy.

Additional Teaching Resource
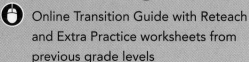
Online Transition Guide with Reteach and Extra Practice worksheets from previous grade levels

ALTERNATE INTERVENTION STRATEGY

Materials: connecting or unit cubes, TRT14 (Grid Paper)

Strategy: Use connecting cubes to model a histogram.

1. Have students work in pairs. Distribute 60 connecting or unit cubes to each pair. Explain to students that they will be making a 3-dimensional display using the cubes.

2. Review the table in the example. Explain that the ages from 0 to 99 have been divided into 5 equal groups, or ranges. The first row shows the age ranges. The second row shows the frequency of values, the number of people within each range.

3. Have pairs construct a bar for each age interval in the table using the connecting cubes. **Ask** How many cubes do you need for the people who are between 0 and 19 years old? [8] How many cubes do you need for the people who are between 20 and 39? [16] 40 and 59? [18] 60 and 79? [15] 80 and 99? [3]

4. Once students have created their displays, ask questions regarding the lengths of the bars in comparison to each other. **Ask** How many people are between 20 and 39 years old? [16] How many people are 59 years old or younger? [8 + 16 + 18 = 42 people] Are more people 39 or younger, or 60 or older? [24 people are 39 or younger, and 18 people are 60 or older, so more people are 39 or younger.]

5. Then have pairs use the grid paper to draw a histogram to display the data. Remind students that there is no space between the bars in a histogram. Together, agree on a title, labels for the axes, and an interval. Have students write and answer a question about the data displayed in their histograms.

Solve a Histogram Problem

Example

The table shows the ages of 60 people who attended a family reunion.

Age (years)	0–19	20–39	40–59	60–79	80–99
Number of People	8	16	18	15	3

a) Draw a histogram to display the information in the table.

Label the x-axis with the age ranges in the table. Choose an appropriate scale and interval for the y-axis. Use the information in the second row of the table to draw the correct height for each bar. Label each axis, and write a title for the histogram.

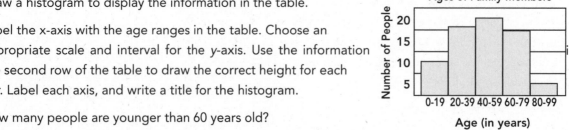

b) How many people are younger than 60 years old?

To find the total, add the number of people in the 0–19, 20–39, and 40–59 age ranges in the histogram: 8 + 16 + 18 = 42.

c) What percent of people are 40 years old or older?
Write a fraction to represent the people who are 40 or older : $\frac{36}{60} = \frac{3}{5}$.
Write the fraction as a percent 60%.

✓ Quick Check
Draw a histogram to display the data. Answer the questions.

1 The table shows the mass of fish caught in a lake one day.

a) Draw a histogram to display this information.

b) How many of the fish have a mass of 2 kg or more? _____

c) What percent of the fish have a mass of 3 kg or more? _____

Mass (kg)	Number of Fish
0–0.9	4
1.0–1.9	7
2.0–2.9	9
3.0–3.9	11
4.0–4.9	9

Practice on Your Own
Draw a histogram to display the data. Answer the questions.

2 The table shows the average number of minutes that 25 students study each night.

a) Draw a histogram to display this information.

b) How many the students spend less than 60 minutes studying?

_____

c) What percent of the students spend 90 minutes or more studying?

_____

Time (min)	Number of Students
0–29	2
30–58	5
60–89	6
90–119	8
120–148	4

Answers

Skill 1

Quick Check

1. $-3, -1, 0, \frac{1}{3}, 2.3$

$-3 \quad -2 \quad -1 \quad 0\frac{1}{3} \quad 1 \quad 2\,2.3\,3$

2. $-2, 0.5, \frac{5}{4}, \frac{8}{3}, 3$

$-3 \quad -2 \quad -1 \quad 0\,0.5\,1\frac{5}{4} \quad 2 \quad \frac{8}{3} \quad 3$

Practice on Your Own

3. $\frac{1}{5}, 0.8, 1.8, \frac{17}{8}, 2.5$

$0\,\frac{1}{5} \quad 0.8\,1 \quad 1.8\,2\frac{17}{8}\,2.5 \quad 3$

4. $\frac{1}{6}, \frac{12}{13}, 1\frac{10}{17}, 2.12, \frac{18}{7}$

$0\,\frac{1}{6} \quad 1\frac{12}{13} \quad 1\frac{10}{17} \quad 2\,2.12\,\frac{18}{7} \quad 3$

Skill 2

Quick Check

1. <   2. <   3. >

Practice on Your Own

4. <	5. <	6. =
7. >	8. <	9. >
10. <	11. =	12. >

Skill 3

Quick Check

1. 3,062.85   2. 3,060   3. 3,063

Practice on Your Own

4. 4,300	5. 12.0	6. 64
7. 400	8. 0.08	9. 110.0

Skill 4

Quick Check

1. 9	2. 64	3. 256
4. 11	5. 4	6. 9

Practice on Your Own

7. 49	8. 9	9. 100
10. 1	11. 36	12. 625
13. 169	14. 16	15. 289
16. 7	17. 3	18. 12
19. 24	20. 8	21. 15
22. 10	23. 20	24. 14

Skill 5

Quick Check

1. 64	2. 1	3. 1,000
4. 3	5. 2	6. 8

Practice on Your Own

7. 27	8. 216	9. 8
10. 729	11. 343	12. 512
13. 3,375	14. 1,728	15. 8,000
16. 6	17. 1	18. 9
19. 11	20. 4	21. 7
22. 100	23. 13	24. 30

Skill 6

Quick Check

1. 16; 39; 62; 62; 63   2. 16
3. −62 and 62   4. −63
5. −63

Practice on Your Own

6. 76; 43; 93; 112; 113; 98; 121; 112
7. 43
8. −112 and 112
9. −121
10. −121

Skill 7

Quick Check

1. >   2. >   3. <

Practice on Your Own

4. <	5. >	6. <
7. >	8. >	9. >
10. <	11. >	12. >

Skill 8

Quick Check

1. 12 **2.** 4 **3.** 0

Practice on Your Own

4. 55 **5.** 8 **6.** 27
7. 62 **8.** 7 **9.** 0
10. 1 **11.** 6 **12.** 69
13. 57 **14.** 13 **15.** 111

Skill 9

Quick Check

1. $1\frac{1}{2}$ **2.** $1\frac{7}{12}$ **3.** $3\frac{2}{3}$

4. $\frac{43}{9}$ **5.** $\frac{44}{7}$ **6.** $\frac{53}{10}$

Practice on Your Own

7. $1\frac{1}{3}$ **8.** $4\frac{4}{5}$ **9.** $1\frac{4}{7}$

10. $2\frac{3}{4}$ **11.** $1\frac{2}{11}$ **12.** 3

13. $2\frac{4}{5}$ **14.** $3\frac{1}{5}$ **15.** $7\frac{1}{2}$

16. $\frac{16}{7}$ **17.** $\frac{31}{9}$ **18.** $\frac{31}{6}$

19. $\frac{77}{12}$ **20.** $\frac{8}{7}$ **21.** $\frac{26}{9}$

22. $\frac{38}{9}$ **23.** $\frac{61}{8}$ **24.** $\frac{60}{7}$

Skill 10

Quick Check

1. $7\frac{17}{20}$ **2.** $4\frac{1}{9}$ **3.** $\frac{13}{35}$

Practice on Your Own

4. $4\frac{13}{28}$ **5.** $8\frac{43}{72}$ **6.** $7\frac{14}{40}$

7. $7\frac{29}{35}$ **8.** $1\frac{11}{36}$ **9.** $3\frac{1}{10}$

Skill 11

Quick Check

1. $\frac{3}{5}$ **2.** $\frac{10}{21}$ **3.** $\frac{1}{16}$

Practice on Your Own

4. $\frac{1}{3}$ **5.** $\frac{1}{21}$ **6.** $\frac{2}{3}$

7. $\frac{3}{50}$ **8.** $\frac{3}{10}$ **9.** $\frac{16}{27}$

10. $\frac{21}{55}$ **11.** $\frac{1}{7}$ **12.** $\frac{5}{16}$

Skill 12

Quick Check

1. $\frac{3}{4}$ **2.** $\frac{1}{2}$ **3.** $2\frac{4}{7}$

Practice on Your Own

4. $1\frac{3}{5}$ **5.** $\frac{1}{9}$ **6.** $\frac{5}{6}$

7. $1\frac{1}{2}$ **8.** $\frac{9}{25}$ **9.** $1\frac{3}{7}$

10. $1\frac{1}{15}$ **11.** $2\frac{1}{10}$ **12.** $1\frac{7}{18}$

Skill 13

Quick Check

1. 72.32 **2.** 83.83 **3.** 13.108

Practice on Your Own

4. 25.893 **5.** 28.07 **6.** 41.58
7. 7.2 **8.** 76.328 **9.** 30.42
10. 43.56 **11.** 83.072 **12.** 190.4
13. 2.618 **14.** 1.892 **15.** 89.25

Skill 14

Quick Check

1. 4.5 **2.** 42 **3.** 12.3

Practice on Your Own

4. 15.4 **5.** 4.7 **6.** 5.6
7. 4.8 **8.** 9.2 **9.** 13.3
10. 0.05 **11.** 2.95 **12.** 4.05
13. 3.25 **14.** 9.2 **15.** 23.7

Skill 15

Quick Check

1. 12 **2.** 36%
3. (a) 63
   (b) 60%

Practice on Your Own

4. 80 **5.** 27.5%
6. $49 **7.** 5%
8. (a) 30 pounds
   (b) 750%

Skill 16

Quick Check

1. m **2.** 5   **3.** 7
4. 2   **5.** +

Practice on Your Own

6. z **7.** 6   **8.** 8
9. –   **10.** $6z$ **11.** 8
12. 2

Skill 17

Quick Check

1. 9   **2.** 17   **3.** 5
4. 5   **5.** 2   **6.** 6

Practice on Your Own

y	$y - 4$	$5y$	$3y + 2$
3	$3 - 4 = -1$	15	11
0	-4	0	2
-2	-6	-10	-4
5	1	25	17
-4	-8	-20	-10

Skill 18

Quick Check

1. No; the x and y terms cannot be combined.
2. Yes; the b terms can be combined.

Practice on Your Own

5. $12x$ **6.** $11m + 16$
7. $-8d + 8$, or $8 - 8d$ **8.** $15j + 8$
9. $-5y - 8$ **10.** $7x + 4$

Skill 19

Quick Check

1. $9y - 6$ **2.** $7 + 48a$ **3.** $16e + 20$

Practice on Your Own

4. $42s + 18$ **5.** $16 - 8r$ **6.** $24 + 12m$
7. $5b - 40$ **8.** $45d + 63$ **9.** $40s - 8$
10. $49 + 49g$ **11.** $20k - 90$ **12.** $36v - 24$
13. $72 + 36w$ **14.** $48n - 64$ **15.** $121p + 55$

Skill 20

Quick Check

1. $4(y + 3)$
2. only common factor is 1
3. $2(8t - 1)$

Practice on Your Own

4. $2(4j + 9)$
5. $4(3s - 7)$
6. only common factor is 1
7. $3(1 - 5g)$
8. only common factor is 1
9. $5(2c + 5)$
10. $7(3x - 2)$
11. $5(2r + 3)$
12. only common factor is 1

Skill 21

Quick Check

1. a) $4(2a - 1)$ **2. c)** $3(4 + y)$

Practice on Your Own

3. d) $2(2n - 5)$ **4. b)** $33d - 66$
5. a) $6(5 + 3p)$ **6. a)** $56r + 16$

Skill 22

Quick Check

1. $\frac{22}{x}$, or $22 \div x$ **2.** $x + 6$, or
3. $x - 13$ **4.** $19x$

Practice on Your Own

5. $72x$ **6.** $\frac{x}{22}$, or $x \div 12$
7. $2x - 8$ **8.** $x + 1.5$
9. $3x - 12$ **10.** $\frac{1}{2}x + 1$

Skill 23

Quick Check

1. $x = 9$ **2.** $x = 8$ **3.** $x = 5$

Practice on Your Own

4. $x = 50$ **5.** $x = \frac{3}{4}$ **6.** $x = 4.5$
7. $x = 4\frac{3}{4}$ **8.** $x = 34$ **9.** $x = 3$

Skill 24

Quick Check

1. False   **2.** True   **3.** False

Practice on Your Own

4. True   **5.** False   **6.** True
7. False

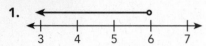

Skill 25

Quick Check

1. (number line: open circle at 6, arrow left; 3 4 5 6 7)
2. (number line: closed circle at 5.5, arrow right; 3 4 5 5.5 6 7)
3. (number line: closed circle at −2, arrow left; −4 −3 −2 −1 0)
4. (number line: open circle at ½, arrow right; 0 ½ 1 2 3 4)
5. (number line: open circle at 11.5, arrow right; 11 11.5 12 13 14 15)
6. (number line: closed circle at 20, arrow left; 18 19 20 21 22)

Practice on Your Own

7. (number line: closed circle at 18, arrow left; 17 18 19 20 21)
8. (number line: open circle at 3¾, arrow left; −3 −2 −1 0 3¾ 1)
9. (number line: closed circle at 12.5, arrow left; 10 11 12 12.5 13 14)
10. (number line: open circle at −6.5, arrow right; −8 −7 −6 −5 −4)
11. (number line: closed circle at 2⅓, arrow right; 0 1 2 2⅓ 3 4)
12. (number line: open circle at 8.6, arrow left; 6 7 8 8.6 9 10)

Skill 26

Quick Check

1. < 2. >
3. $x > 4$ 4. $x \le 10$

Practice on Your Own

5. = 6. >
7. $x \ge 25$ 8. $x < 35$
9. $x \le 80$ 10. $x > 24$

Skill 27

Quick Check

1. 5 to 6, 5 : 6, $\frac{5}{6}$ 2. 2 to 3, 2 : 3, $\frac{2}{3}$

Practice on Your Own

3. 1 : 4 4. 5 : 2 5. 1 : 7
6. 4 : 1 7. 2 : 1 8. 5 : 18

Skill 28

Quick Check

1. No
2. Yes
3. No; samples: 3 : 4, 9 : 12
4. Yes; samples: 6 to 14, 9 to 21
5. No; samples: 3 to 5, 12 to 20

Practice on Your Own

5. No; samples: 3 to 5, 12 to 20
6. Yes; samples: $\frac{4}{10}$, $\frac{6}{15}$
7. No; samples: $\frac{2}{9}$, $\frac{18}{81}$
8. Yes; samples: $\frac{2}{16}$, $\frac{3}{24}$
9. No; samples: 2 : 3, 8 : 12
10. Yes; samples: 42 : 16, 63 : 24
11. Yes; samples: 8 : 30, 12 : 45
12. No; samples: 1 to 3, 2 to 6
13. No; samples: 5 to 1, 60 to 12
14. No; samples: 3 to 8, 12 to 32

Skill 29

Quick Check

1. 9 mi/h 2. Ms. Lu

Practice on Your Own

3. white: $0.85 per lb; red: $0.89 per lb
4. Write-On: $0.50 per pen; Ink: $0.50 per pen
5. Jenna
6. salami

Skill 30

Quick Check

1. (4, 4) 2. (7, 6)
3. (5, 0) 4. (0, 3)

Practice on Your Own

5. (5, 3) 6. (2, 8)

7.

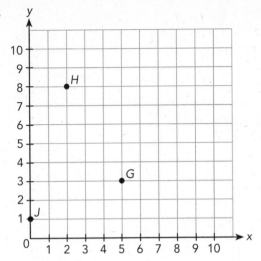

8.

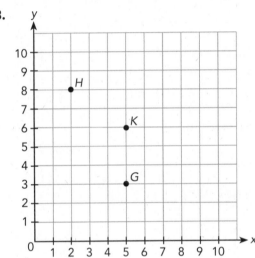

Quick Check

1. $\overline{GJ}$ and $\overline{HI}$
2. $\overline{LM}$ and $\overline{ON}$; $\overline{LO}$ and $\overline{MN}$
3. $\overline{QR}$ and $\overline{QT}$; $\overline{QR}$ and $\overline{RS}$; $\overline{TS}$ and $\overline{QT}$; $\overline{TS}$ and $\overline{RS}$
4. $\overline{BC}$ and $\overline{BA}$

Practice on Your Own

5. $\overline{CD}$ and $\overline{FE}$
   $\overline{CD}$ and $\overline{DE}$, $\overline{FE}$ and $\overline{DE}$

Skill 34

Quick Check

1. scalene
2. isosceles
3. equilateral

Practice on Your Own

4. isosceles
5. equilateral
6. scalene
7. scalene

Skill 35

Quick Check

1. obtuse
2. right
3. acute

Practice on Your Own

4. acute
5. obtuse
6. right
7. acute

Skill 31

Quick Check

1. $288
2. 60
3. $248.40
4. 146.2

Practice on Your Own

5. 7.84
6. 648
7. $702
8. 3,333
9. 35
10. $132.50

Skill 32

Quick Check

1. acute angle
2. right angle
3. acute angle
4. obtuse angle

Practice on Your Own

5. obtuse angle
6. acute angle
7. obtuse angle
8. obtuse angle
9. obtuse angle
10. acute angle

Skill 36

Quick Check

1. rhombus
2. trapezoid
3. rectangle

Practice on Your Own

4. parallelogram
5. square
6. rhombus

Skill 37

Quick Check

1. 12°
2. 90°
3. 138°

Practice on Your Own

4. 60°
5. 130°
6. 175°

Skill 38

Quick Check

1.

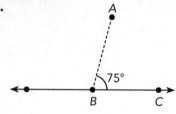

2.

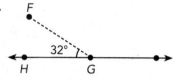

Practice on Your Own

4.

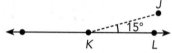

5.

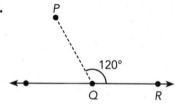

Skill 39

Quick Check

1.

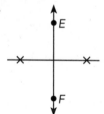

2.

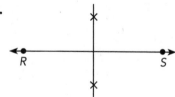

Practice on Your Own

3.

4.

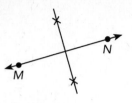

Skill 40

Quick Check

1. 390 cm²	**2.** 96 in.²	**3.** 198 m²
378 cm³	64 in.³	108 m³

Practice on Your Own

4. 190 ft²	**5.** 126 yd²	**6.** 600 in.²
150 ft³	81 yd³	1,000 in.³
7. 6 m		

Skill 41

Quick Check

1. 240 in.²	**2.** 208 cm²	**3.** 456 yd²

Practice on Your Own

4. 363 m²	**5.** 644 in.²	**6.** 2,220 ft²
7. 448 cm²		

Skill 42

Quick Check

1. a) 2,826 cm²	**2. a)** 12.56 ft²
b) 188.4 cm	**b)** 12.56 ft

Practice on Your Own

3. a) 379.94 in.²	**4. a)** 200.96 m²
b) 69.08 in.	**b)** 50.24 m

Skill 43

Quick Check

1. square pyramid	**2.** rectangular prism
3. triangular prism	

Practice on Your Own

4. triangular prism	**5.** cube
6. square pyramid	**7.** rectangular prism

Skill 44

Quick Check

1. 37	**2.** 13.4	**3.** 14.24

Practice on Your Own

4. 47.13 mi/h	**5.** 40.86 lb

Skill 45

Quick Check

1. 98
2. 32
3. 6
4. 433.5

Practice on Your Own

5. 1.5 inches
6. 80.5

Skill 46

Quick Check

1.

Number of Vacation Days Taken	0	1	2	3	4	5	6	7	8	9
Number of Workers	1	0	0	0	1	3	5	0	1	1

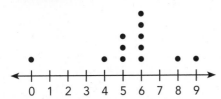

Number of Vacation Days Taken

Practice on Your Own

2.

Number of Paintings Created	2	3	4	5	6	7	8	9	10	11	12
Number of Students	3	2	4	4	3	0	2	1	0	0	1

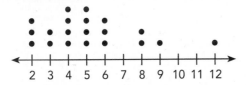

Number of Paintings Created

Skill 47

Quick Check

1. $\frac{1}{4}$
2. 70%

Practice on Your Own

3. 28%
4. $\frac{4}{5}$
5. $\frac{1}{3}$
6. 68%

Skill 48

Quick Check

1. 80%
2. 11.11%
3. 125%

Practice on Your Own

4. 48%
5. 208.33%
6. 170%
7. 75%
8. 128.57%
9. 33.33%
10. 25%
11. 66.67%
12. 240%

Skill 49

Quick Check

1. $\frac{19}{25}$
2. $\frac{21}{100}$
3. $1\frac{6}{25}$
4. 2.99
5. 0.423
6. 0.08

Practice on Your Own

7. $1\frac{12}{25}$
8. $\frac{13}{500}$
9. $\frac{13}{20}$
10. 4.13
11. 0.093
12. 0.001

Skill 50

Quick Check

1. a) $\frac{2}{5}$
   b) 40%

Practice on Your Own

2. a) $\frac{9}{40}$
   b) 23%

Skill 51

Quick Check

1. a)

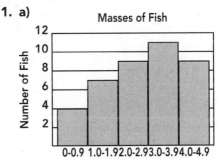

Masses of Fish

b) 29
c) 50%

2. a)

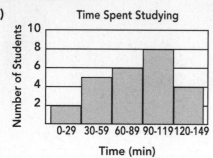

Time Spent Studying

b) 7

c) 48%